D0736217

# SUBSIDIARITY GOVERNANCE

## Previous Publications

(ed. with A. Brugnoli) *Government, Governance and Welfare Reform. Structural Changes and Subsidiarity in Italy and Britain* [forthcoming]

(ed.) (2010) *Far bene e fare il bene. Contributi e materiali per una storia del welfare in Lombardia*

(ed. with R. Cucca) (2010) *Innovare la democrazia. Teorie ed esperienze di deliberazione pubblica*

(2004) *The Principle of Subsidiarity and the European Citizenship*

(2004) *Congregazioni religiose e sviluppo in Lombardia tra Otto e Novecento*

(ed.) (2002) *Work as Key to the Social Question. The Great Social and Economic Transformations and the Subjective Dimension of Work*

# SUBSIDIARITY GOVERNANCE

## THEORETICAL AND EMPIRICAL MODELS

Edited by

*Alessandro Colombo*

SUBSIDIARITY GOVERNANCE
Copyright © Alessandro Colombo, 2012.

First published in 2012 by
PALGRAVE MACMILLAN®
in the United States—a division of St. Martin's Press LLC,
175 Fifth Avenue, New York, NY 10010.

Where this book is distributed in the UK, Europe and the rest of the world,
this is by Palgrave Macmillan, a division of Macmillan Publishers Limited,
registered in England, company number 785998, of Houndmills,
Basingstoke, Hampshire RG21 6XS.

Palgrave Macmillan is the global academic imprint of the above companies
and has companies and representatives throughout the world.

Palgrave® and Macmillan® are registered trademarks in the United States,
the United Kingdom, Europe and other countries.

ISBN: 978–0–230–33869–2

Library of Congress Cataloging-in-Publication Data

Subsidiarity governance : theoretical and empirical models / edited by
Alessandro Colombo.
    p. cm.
    ISBN 978–0–230–33869–2 (hardback)
    1. Lombardy (Italy)—Politics and government. 2. Decentralization in
government—Italy—Lombardy. 3. Central-local government relations—
Italy—Lombardy. 4. Subsidiarity. I. Colombo, Alessandro, 1966–

JN5690.L622S83 2012
320.80945'2—dc23                                          2011027237

A catalogue record of the book is available from the British Library.

Design by Newgen Imaging Systems (P) Ltd., Chennai, India.

First edition: January 2012

10 9 8 7 6 5 4 3 2 1

Printed in the United States of America.

*To Maddalena, Filippo, Caterina, Cecilia*

# CONTENTS

*List of Figures*                                                    ix

*List of Tables*                                                     xi

*List of Interviewees Quoted in the Volume*                        xiii

*Acknowledgments*                                                    xv

*Introduction*                                                     xvii

## Part I    The Model of Governance

1   Principle of Subsidiarity and Lombardy: Theoretical
    Background and Empirical Implementation                          3
    *Alessandro Colombo*

2   Subsidiarity and the New Governance: Reflections on
    the Lombard Experience                                          19
    *Lester M. Salamon*

3   A Hornet's Nest or the Climax of the Change of
    Regime? The Dilemmas of Creating Regions in
    Eastern and Central Europe                                      31
    *Gyula Horváth*

4   An Unfinished Journey—Lombardy on the
    Road to Decentralization                                        51
    *Balázs Lóránd*

5   A View from the Antipodes: Comparing the Lombard
    and New Zealand Ways of Governance                              73
    *Philip McDermott*

## Part II    Policy Sectors

6   Subsidiarity and Education in Lombardy:
    Limits and Possibilities                                       113
    *Charles L. Glenn*

7 Regional Governance of Health Services in
  Lombardy                                                     135
  *Helen Haugh*

8 Subsidiarity, Proximity, and Innovation                     147
  *Michael Kitson*

9 Social Housing and Subsidiarity in the Lombard
  Model of Governance                                          157
  *Gerard Van Bortel*


*Notes on the Contributors*                                    171

*Index*                                                        175

# Figures

4.1 Differences between the Quasi-Market Structure
and the Subsidiarity Model      59

4.2 The Lombard Model of Governance      60

5.1 Intergovernmental Arrangements, New Zealand and
Lombardy      99

9.1 Italian Social Housing in an International Perspective      158

# Tables

1.1    Lombard Region School Subsidies    13

3.1    Changes in the Number of Regional Administrative
Units in Eastern and Central European Countries    33

3.2    The Most Significant Data of NUTS 2 Units in
Eastern and Central Europe    39

3.3    The Weight of Capital Cities in Eastern and Central
Europe, as Percentage of National Total, 2004    41

5.1    Comparing Governance Arrangements,
New Zealand and Lombardy    100

6.1    Beneficiaries and Amount Received    127

9.1    Indicators on Housing Owned by Public Actors in
Lombardy    160

# Interviewees Quoted in the Volume

## Chapter 4

Piero Bassetti, Globus et Locus Foundation
Alberto Ceriani, Éupolis Lombardia
Bruno Dente, Politecnico di Milano—Polytechnic University of Milan
Antonio Intiglietta, Federazione Compagnia delle Opere Lombardia—Federation of Compagnia delle Opere in Lombardy
Federico Rappelli, Éupolis Lombardia
Giancarlo Rovati, Università Cattolica del Sacro Cuore—Catholic University of the Sacred Heart
Neva Sbrissa, Lombardy Regional Government
Lorenza Violini, Università degli Studi di Milano—The University of Milan
Giorgio Vittadini, Fondazione per la Sussidiarietà—Foundation for Subsidiarity

## Chapter 6

Giuseppe Colosio, Ufficio scolastico regionale della Lombardia—National Office for Schools in Lombardy
Roberto Albonetti, Lombardy Regional Government

## Chapter 7

Paolo Vignali, Éupolis Lombardia

# ACKNOWLEDGMENTS

This book owes much to many; it's the result of the collective effort of people willing to better understand experiences and freely share opinions.

I would like to express my profound gratitude to all the authors for the time, skills, and effort that they devoted to it.

I am extremely indebted to the Lombardy Regional Government and my institute (IReR—Lombardy Regional Institute for Research now Éupolis Lombardia), to Alberto Brugnoli, director, and all my colleagues for giving me the full support and freedom to organize and develop the project.

Maria Chiara Cattaneo holds the merit of successfully coordinating both the project and the book; I am deeply grateful for her help.

Thanks to Max Beber for his suggestions, which were always valuable and objective, and to Eleanor de Veras for her patient help.

I am also very grateful to all those who accepted to be interviewed but are not quoted; their names are listed below.

Tommaso Agasisti, Guido Bardelli, Francesco Bargiggia, Elena Besozzi, Franco Biasoni, Lucia Boccacin, Adolfo Boffi, Carlo Borelli, Francesca Borgato, Elio Borsani, Daniele Botti, Alberto Bramanti, Luciano Caffini, Pietro Calascibetta, Gregoria Cannarozzo, Marco Carabelli, Leonardo Cascitelli, Lucia Castellana, Carlo Cerami, Stefano Chiappelli, Gianluigi Coghi, Daniela Colombo, Maria Grazia Colombo, Giovanni Cominelli, Luciano Consolati, Roberto Cosentina, Felice Crema, Elvira Cretella, Lucia Cusmano, Alessia Damonte, Armando De Crinito, Gabriele Delotti, Benedetto Di Rienzo, Chiara Fanali, Matteo Foppa Pedretti, Andrea Franzetti, Furio Gramatica, Onorato Grassi, Domenico Ippolito, Valter Izzo, Francesco La Teana, Domenico Lenoci, Giuseppe Losio, Luigi Macchi, Mario Maestri, Stefano Malfatti, Maria Luisa Mancusi, Leonardo Marabini, Giovanni Marseguerra, Bruno Marzia, Luca Merlino, Andrea Monteduro, Valeria Negri, Patrizia Neri, Carlo Nicora, Mario Nova, Eliana Pacchiani, Raffaela Paggi, Francesca Pasquini, Andrea

Perrone, Renata Rava, Maria Pia Redaelli, Alessandro Ronchi, Anna Maria Rossato, Giovanna Rossi, Maria Grazia Santagati, Diego Sempio, Davide Sironi, Lorella Sossi, Leo Spinelli, Giuseppe Strada, Renato Ugo, Sergio Urbani, Giuliano Vecchi, Stefano Vignati, Giuseppe Vivace, Loris Zaffra, Franco Zinna.

# INTRODUCTION

Over the last fifteen years, a distinctive experience of government has been accumulated in Lombardy. A unique experiment in Italy, the reform process has included a range of political, legislative, and administrative initiatives that have resulted in a political practice inspired by the so-called "principle of subsidiarity" (Brugnoli and Vittadini, 2009).

This experience of government has been designed and developed in an incremental way rather than systematically, and the path of reform has been certainly characterized by contradictory elements. Over time the awareness of implementing a new "model" of governance has been progressively raised and subsidiarity has been increasingly recognized as the theoretical paradigm of the model.

The distinctiveness of the Lombard model relies on the subsidiarity principle, which is able to challenge some of the fundamental patterns of innovative models of governance, that is, the quasi markets. This is a critical reflection process still in progress that will be detailed in this book.

The already-existing literature describing the subsidiarity-informed experience of government in Lombardy and the institutional innovation carried out by the regional government is mainly domestic (see Colombo 2008, Brugnoli and Vittadini 2009). In particular, IReR (Lombardy Regional Institute for Research—now "Éupolis Lombardia, Institute for Research, Statistics, and Training) has played a key role in enhancing the analysis of the model at both the national and international levels. The action of IReR has constantly been supported by the Lombardy Regional Government, which is strongly committed to widening the analytical horizon by taking an active part in the international academic debate over different governance experiences. Since 2007, IReR has multiplied its relations with international scholars and institutions, that is, institutes of research, universities, and think tanks, especially in Europe and the United States. Having in mind to provide an initial understanding of the Lombard model based on the concepts of trust, freedom, and responsibility and spread it at international level, IReR has organized a series of seminars and conferences[1] every year. Each seminar is an opportunity to listen, discuss, and compare views in order to consolidate the governance practices and principles that distinguish the Lombard model of governance. Different approaches and perspectives advanced by the external debaters contributed to broaden the analysis of the model.[2]

In 2010 IReR has implemented a research *Lombard Model: International Assessments. Evaluation and Ideas of a Subsidiarity-Inspired Way of Governance* that aimed at exploring to what extent the Lombard experience can be improved by collecting authoritative and evidence-based analysis of its model of governance written by prominent international scholars and experts in the field of governance. The chapters presented in this volume are each author's "structured reactions" to the Lombard model, achieved through a program of readings and direct contacts and interviews taking place in Milan. The overall purpose of this volume is twofold. First, it intends delineating the key elements and main features of a subsidiarity-informed model of governance as it has been implemented in Lombardy. Therefore, it ambitiously tries to outline an analytical framework that could be applied to other subsidiarity-informed models of governance worldwide. Second, on the basis of the last fifteen years' Lombard experience of government, the volume will attempt to identify what are the challenges ahead in order to implement a genuine subsidiarity-informed governance.

An important premise is needed. All the chapters presented in the book are based on a review of a set of documents provided to the authors by officials in the IReR; on a series of interviews arranged for the authors by IReR officials in January 2010; and other conversations with staff and leaders of others stakeholders and associations. Given the limited empirical base on which these comments are based, they must be understood as best preliminary hypotheses rather than settled findings. As such they can point the way to the further fact-finding that is still needed.

## NOTES

1. See http://www.irer.it/eventi/governancegiugno2007.pdf/, accessed on September 23, 2011.
2. In 2009, IReR organized a series of video interviews. Several international experts were asked to give their opinion on Lombard region. The

video interviews are available at http://www.irer.it/home_en/home_2
/?searchterm=videointerviews, accessed on September 23, 2011.

## References

Brugnoli, A., and G. Vittadini (2009) *Subsidiarity: Positive Anthropology and Social Organization. Foundations for a New Conception of State and Market and Key Points of the Experience in Lombardy* (Milan: Guerini).

Colombo, A. (2008) "The 'Lombardy model': Subsidiarity-informed regional governance" in *Social Policy & Administration*, 42(2), 177–96.

# Part I

# THE MODEL OF GOVERNANCE

# 1

# Principle of Subsidiarity and Lombardy: Theoretical Background and Empirical Implementation

## Alessandro Colombo

This introductory chapter frames the main themes of the book's individual contributions, by providing the reader with the historical and analytical fundamentals of a key philosophical principle, that of subsidiarity, and with the stylized facts of governance in the Lombard region in northern Italy.

## 1.1. What is the Principle of Subsidiarity?

### 1.1.1. Definition

The subsidiarity principle states that in all forms of human coexistence, no organization must dominate and replace other weaker or smaller ones in the exercise of the latter's functions. On the contrary, the moral duty of larger and more powerful social bodies is to bring help (from Latin *subsidium afferre*) to the smaller ones in the fulfillment of aspirations freely determined at this smaller level, rather than imposed from above.

In spite of its relatively recent popularity in the wider public debate, subsidiarity has deep cultural, philosophical, theological, and political roots (Rinella 1999; Hoffmann 1993; Duret, 2000; Follesdal 2000), often linked to Catholic social tradition. Indeed, its most frequently referenced occurrence is the in following passage from *Quadragesimo Anno*, the encyclical issued in 1931 by Pope Pius IX:

> It is a fundamental principle of social philosophy, fixed and unchangeable, that one should not withdraw from individuals and commit to the community what they can accomplish by their own enterprise and industry. So, too, it is an injustice and at the same time a grave evil and a disturbance of right order, to transfer to the larger and higher collectivity functions which can be performed and provided for by lesser and subordinate bodies. In as much as every social activity should, by its very nature, prove a help to members of the body social, it should never destroy or absorb them [ ... ]. The supreme authority of the State ought, therefore, to let subordinate groups handle matters and concerns of lesser importance, which would otherwise dissipate its efforts greatly. Thereby the State will more freely, powerfully and effectively do all those things that belong to it alone because it alone can do them: directing, watching, urging, restraining as occasion requires and necessity demands. Therefore, those in power should be sure that the more perfectly a graduated order is kept among the various associations, in observance of the principle of "subsidiarity function," the stronger social authority and effectiveness will be, the happier and more prosperous the condition of the State. (Quoted in Carlen, 1990, vol. 3, p. 428; see also Mulcahy, 1967, p. 762)

In governance terms, subsidiarity implies that political structures, such as the nation-state or regional governments, should only intervene when this is necessary to protect the common good, and to perform those tasks that cannot be effectively carried out at a more immediate, or local, level. Thus subsidiarity emphasizes the importance of endowing individuals with autonomy and with the resources necessary to fulfill a responsibility for developing and delivering the services they need; it interprets local structures—the family, the church, community groups, and voluntary associations—as mediating structures that empower individuals, and represent and communicate their interests; and it has become primarily associated with efforts to engage a wide variety of social actors in addressing societal problems, and with the empowerment of democratic institutions (Barber, 2005).

### 1.1.2. The Fortune of the "European" Concept of Subsidiarity

As a result of the debate started within the European Union in connection with the single market and monetary union projects, subsidiarity is probably best known as a criterion for assigning competences to different institutional levels of government. Thus, for example, subsidiarity was explicitly invoked in 1991 by the Maastricht Treaty in article 3B (now article 5.3. of the Treaty on the European Union as amended by the Treaty of Lisbon):

> The Community shall act within the limit of the powers conferred upon it by this Treaty and of the objectives assigned to it therein.
>
> In areas which do not follow within its exclusive competence, the Community shall take action, in accordance with the principle of subsidiarity, only if and in so far as the objectives of the proposed action cannot be sufficiently achieved by the Member States and can therefore, by reason of the scale or effects of the proposed action, be better achieved by the Community.
>
> Any action by the Community shall not go beyond what is necessary to achieve the objectives of this Treaty. (Maastricht Treaty, article 3B)

The high and contentious profile of subsidiarity in the European context has led to an unfortunate narrowing in the analytical scope of the concept: typically, supporters of European integration have stressed the technocratic dimension of subsidiarity—those "reasons of scale and effect" that may on occasion counsel the pooling or centralization of policy competences. Conversely, Euroskeptics have used this criterion as a tool of political compromise, used defensively in bargaining over successive treaties and Commission initiatives (Carozza, 2003, p. 42).

In both cases, subsidiarity is considered as a mere a principle regulating the distribution of public powers; this is a correct, but somewhat limited, interpretation of a principle whose roots are not primarily institutional, but rather anthropological and socio-philosophical.

### 1.1.3. Anthropological Root

Subsidiarity, in fact, relates to the constitutive nature of the individual and its relationship with society and politics.

Human beings are intrinsically, constitutionally in search of happiness and fulfillment. This innate desire interacts with the practical and fundamental needs of everyday life, but at the same time it transcends them. Human dignity lies in this dynamic of desire that expresses itself in the realm of the finite despite being infinite. Driven by such desire, individuals freely pursue their own fulfillment, developing relationships of social cooperation (beginning with the family) in the process of doing so. Recognizing the primacy of the actions of the individual, and the social bodies immediately derived from those individual actions, implies a complex and dynamic interpretation of sociality: starting from the family and the closest community relationships, society evolves toward the most complex and widespread political institutions according to a continuum where the forms and rules of these relationships change, but where the fundamental value of the individual as beginning and end of the action remains essential. All forms of social relations are then founded upon the necessity to enable all human beings to become fulfilled (idea of the "common good"); they emerge not to replace the free efforts of the individuals, but to support (from Latin *subsidium afferre*) them in their efforts. Subsidiarity demands that personal freedom be promoted in a way that is suitable to its multiplicity of forms and levels.

### 1.1.4. "Vertical" and "Horizontal" Subsidiarity

It is important to distinguish between two quite distinct meanings of the principle of subsidiarity, which have been employed in the current debate, at times without sufficient differentiation.

The first one, more popular and already mentioned above with reference to the European Union's debate, is called "vertical subsidiarity" (Rinella, 1999, p. 3 ff.) and concerns the correct relationship between the various levels of sovereignty and institutional competence. In local, regional, national, and supranational authorities, higher levels must not replace the lower ones, but help them. Higher/larger institutions can protect the lower/smaller ones in two ways: (a) via active intervention and support, when the lower institutions alone are not able to guarantee the adequate continuation of the social purpose in question; (b) by guaranteeing, and respecting, the autonomy of lower-level organizations whenever they are capable of achieving the given purpose.

The second meaning, closer in some ways to the original meaning of the term, is called "horizontal subsidiarity." This refers to the sharing of competences, functions, and services between the public and social subjects and recognizes the priority of society and intermediate bodies over the state. The crucial potential flowing from this acception of subsidiarity is the opportunity that it creates for social interactions and organizations to emerge in forms quite different from those typically associated with the modern state. From the standpoint of horizontal subsidiarity, a "public" function does not necessarily need to be carried out by a state entity; to the contrary, public bodies exist to optimize society's ability to answer its own needs. The state exists not to replace society but to carry out public functions or provide support only when society alone is not capable of looking after itself. In such perspective, intermediate social bodies inhabiting the social space between individual citizens and public institutions, from family to associations, from corporate firms to nonprofit organizations, acquire a new role and significance, paving the way for a radical overhaul of the current concept of the modern state.

### 1.1.5. A Long History

As anticipated earlier, the constituent analytical parts of the concept of subsidiarity long predate the term's appearance in political discourse. The nodes of the relationship between power and legitimacy, between the individual and the state, between freedom and common good have always represented a fertile crossroads for political and philosophical thought. Yet even in the closely woven fabric of Western thought on these themes, it is possible to pick out threads connecting subsidiarity's most ancient premises to contemporary conceptual expositions and practical applications of the principle.

Aristotle's *Politics* set out a vision of the *polis* as an organic whole made up of different parts. This unity is not the mere gathering together of indistinct, anonymous, parts (like the sheep of a flock), but the result of an interplay of the individual, personal, responsibilities of human beings who are uniquely able to understand and to distinguish between good and bad; right and wrong; and are, therefore, able to dialogue:

> Man alone of the animals possesses speech. The mere voice, it is true, can indicate pain and pleasure, and therefore is possessed by the other animals as well (for their nature has been developed so far as to have sensations of what is painful and pleasant and to indicate those sensations to one another), but speech is designed to indicate the advantageous and the harmful, and therefore also the right and the wrong; for it is the special property of man in distinction from the other animals that he alone has perception of good and bad and right and wrong and the other moral qualities, and it is partnership in these things that makes a household and a city-state. (Aristotles, Polics. Book One)

The *polis* is an irreplaceable principle of unity and purpose, its wholeness given by the composition of different parts, each of which exerts its own specific functions. The *polis* alone is a self-sufficient, complete organism; within it we do not discern an indistinct whole, but rather a clear articulation of levels and tasks.

> The state is also prior by nature to the individual; for if each individual when separate is not self-sufficient, he must be related to the whole state as other parts are to their whole, while a man who is incapable of entering into partnership, or who is so self-sufficing that he has no need to do so, is no part of a state, so that he must be either a lower animal or a god. (Aristotles, Polics. Book One)

Starting from the Aristotelian acknowledgement that man is by nature a social animal, Thomas Aquinas (1225–1274) underlines that the political community assists each member not only in securing the material necessities "to live" ("such as those produced by the many industries that are found in a state, and which the family could not produce"), but also in securing the spiritual goods needed to "live well"—including "public authority, which, by the threat of punishment, holds in check the intemperance of those youth that paternal admonition would not be sufficient to correct."

More importantly, Aquinas warns that the political community, or the family, only possesses "a unity of order and this is not an absolute unity" (Aquinas, 1946, p. 174). This implies that the constituent parts of this whole can engage in spheres of action that are distinct from that of the whole (in Aquinas's metaphor, "The soldier may carry out actions that are not those of the entire army.").

Aquinas thus embraces Aristotle's primacy of the community, but tempers it by highlighting the importance of the individuality of those taking part in social life. He recognizes that the functions of the various levels are at the same time complementary and distinct, so that public authority may intervene with an auxiliary function where, for example, family authority is shown to be wanting.

In his reflections on the structuring of society and its relationship with the forms of political sovereignty, Johannes Althusius (1563ca.–1638) stressed in particular the remarkable importance of intermediate social bodies in defining the relationship between the individual and the state: "For families, cities, and provinces existed by nature prior to realms, and gave birth to them" (Althusius, 1603, n. 3). In this context the supreme sovereignty of the state with respect to the intermediate bodies finds its justification and its limit only in the pursuit of the interests that belong to the general association of the people. "The king represents the people not the people the king

[ ... ]. Whence the supreme monarch is required to give an account of his administration, is not permitted for his own pleasure to alienate or diminish the provinces, cities, or towns of his realm, and can even be deposed" (Athusius, 1603, n. 24).

Elements of the principle of subsidiarity are also evident in the foundations of the modern liberal view of the state, laid by John Locke (1632–1704). Locke traced the origin of political authority to the voluntary delegation by individuals of certain personal prerogatives and powers. Precisely because it is free and intentional, this delegation cannot be absolute, but remains proportioned and limited to the capacity of the state to meet the specific objectives set by its citizens at the moment of its genesis. In this form of "negative" subsidiarity, the citizen has a guarantee of noninterference by the state in all areas that do not constitute objectives of the state itself (Locke, 1956, pp. 64–66).

Subsidiarity can also be recognized in the empirical analysis of associations conducted by Alexis de Tocqueville (1805–1859), who saw them as fundamental, structural forms of democracy. De Tocqueville's exploration into the life of the nascent American democracy represents one of the first clear insights into the constitution of the modern forms of political association and social participation. He was impressed by the number of associations that Americans established:

> Americans of all ages, all conditions, and all dispositions constantly form associations [ ... ] Wherever at the head of some new undertaking you see the government in France, or a man of rank in England, in the United States you will be sure to find an association. (Tocqueville, 1954: 114)

The French philosopher emphasized the importance of those associative experiences, exalting young America's capacity to cope "from below" with constantly changing social needs, securing—in the process of doing so—both the development of the spiritual capacities of its individual citizens, and harnessing their free initiative. Yet Tocqueville could also foresee that, with the increasing complexity of modern times, the state could risk overruling people's primary responsibility, colonizing and taking over all the tasks that individuals could otherwise have achieved with their own capabilities and with the art of gathering in associations:

> It is easy to foresee that the time is drawing near when man will be less and less able to produce, by himself alone, the commonest necessaries

of life. The task of the governing power will therefore perpetually increase, and its very efforts will extend it every day. The more it stands in the place of associations, the more will individuals, losing the notion of combining together, require its assistance: these are causes and effects that unceasingly create each other. (Tocqueville, 1954: 117)

On similar lines, John Stuart Mill (1806–1873) developed further the liberal perspective on the relationship between political power and individuals. Freedom represents an insuperable limit for the exercise of the authority of the state, whenever faced with individual choices that do not harm the freedom of others. Conversely, individual freedom and freedom of association carry the duty not to make this space of freedom an opportunity for action rather than indifference, to the mutual advantage of those interacting by means of persuasion and education rather than coercion (Mill, 1903: esp. 60–62, 85–86).

### 1.1.6. Not "against" the State

A common denominator of these theories is that the value of the political system stems from the free, responsible, and cooperative actions of individuals (single or associated), and not vice versa: it is not the political system that gives individuals their dignity and capability to contribute to their own and their fellow citizens' welfare. Political authority has the duty and the right to respect this priority, and therefore to intervene in helping autonomous initiatives by society's members. It also carries the responsibility to guarantee equal opportunities, and respect of the rules.

As Salamon rightly points out in this book:

> This approach goes well beyond the neoliberal ideology that has inspired much of the recent government-reform efforts throughout the world. In particular, while seeking to engage social actors other than the state, it is not antistate. Rather, it promotes a new role for the state, one that acknowledges explicitly the need for a collaborative approach to solving public problems. (Infra Salamon, chapter 2, page 17 in this book)

Subsidiarity sees the state as a mere regulatory *instrument*, not as the *actor* of the social action, let alone the creator of the well-being of its citizens. Governance means not so much taking direct initiative as controlling and helping those who are originally authorized to take action. In this perspective the typically modern dividing line between a public sphere, which is the state's remit, and a private sphere, seen as society's remit, becomes blurred. The modern state in continental Europe has developed by progressively "absorbing" in its remit all public spheres and preexisting autonomous institutions (Poggi, 1990). In the nineteenth century, notably in France and Italy, the state became the only protagonist of the public common good, as opposed to private societal interests, deemed as necessarily partial and conflicting. Only the state was capable of pursuing the public good. Therefore, it was given the monopoly of all public functions, such as education, health care, and social security (Colombo and Zaninelli, 1998). As a result, up until recent times, the majority of Europeans were used to consider the expression "public" as synonymous with "of the state."

The original meaning of horizontal subsidiarity implies full acknowledgement of the *public* contributions of *private* actors. If the public role were simply bestowed by the state upon social organizations' activities, it would mean that once again the state (or whatever other public power) arrogates to itself the monopoly of the public functions.

Subsidiarity is neither just externalization of public services to private/nonprofit actors, nor simply a variant of public–private partnership (PPP). By recognizing the original supremacy of families and social bodies, subsidiarity rests on much deeper foundations—trust in the positive desire, which is an innate human characteristic. It is the very idea of *trust* that opens the way to a new idea of the state. The orthodox concept of state rests on the "Hobbesian" suspicion of the negative effects of individual desires. In this perspective, the state is the only power able to balance individual wishes and the "common good." On the contrary, subsidiarity puts trust in the person's original and positive capability to directly pursue the common good (Donati, 2007).

Of the three forms of regulation described by Polyani (social reciprocity, monetary exchange, and hierarchical redistribution), subsidiarity can be linked to the first one, as it informs relations neither on the basis of utility (benefits/costs) as the market does, nor on the basis of command, which is typical of the state; rather, the defining feature of subsidiarity-informed social relations is the mutual human fulfillment of those participating in them. Therefore, subsidiarity is strictly linked to the concept of solidarity, insofar as it develops through interpersonal reciprocity (Donati, 2005).

## 1.2. THE LOMBARD EXPERIENCE

It seems useful to conclude this introductory chapter with a selection of stylized facts—both structural and governance-related—about the northern Italian region of Lombardy, whose experiences and experiments in subsidiarity-inspired governance are critically examined in the chapters collected in this volume.

Subsidiarity ran through the ultimately successful regional demands for greater decentralization of governance in Italy, which intensified from the early 1990s after several decade during which the regional aspirations of the 1948 Republican Constitution had lain dormant. The reform of the constitution's Title V eventually granted Italy's regions a wider normative and financial autonomy; in exploiting this enhanced policy space, subsidiarity provided an original legitimacy for policies not dissimilar from those pursued elsewhere, and inspired a number of policy experiments, which contribute to give Lombardy's subsidiarity-informed governance its originality (Colombo, 2008).

At the level of legitimacy, Lombardy's reforms have been seen as means to integrate and coordinate the region's action with the activities of the rest of society, rather than as public-service productivity strategies.

In reforming the welfare system, the Lombardy Regional Government attempted to transcend mere outsourcing, and opted instead to retain control over regulation, programming, and financing, while devolving to autonomous bodies the management and delivery of services. On the demand side, the reforms have promoted freedom of choice for citizens and families.

Lombardy has been at the forefront of this process, especially in welfare policies. The most remarkable outcome is that the initial gap between supply and demand of welfare services (e.g., for the disabled, families, the elderly) has been bridged over a ten-year period.

A regional law adopted in 1999 laid out the principles of family support, and succeeded in overcoming the fragmentation of services (De Carli, 2005). Just as importantly, the "subsidiarity by projects" vision has stimulated the autonomous response of civil society: The region provides financial support for hundreds of projects presented by families' associations, creating family support services such as micronurseries.

At the level of intermediate bodies, the region has granted financial aids to thousands of Catholic youth centers—which have a centuries-old tradition in Lombardy—and private nursery schools. Wherever possible, according to state law, the region has opted for fiscal benefits instead of direct funding. For instance, it abolished the regional tax on business revenues as well as regional automobile tax for not for profit organizations and institutions.

### 1.2.1. Education

For the first time in Italy, the regional government introduced subsidies for those families sending children to nonstate schools, supporting freedom of choice in the education of children. School fees are thus (partially) refunded on the basis of criteria such as the family's gross income, number of children, and exceptional hardship. Over 50,000 applications are submitted each year, and €40 million allocated (see Table 1.1.). The subsidies have become quite popular in the region although they have not, on average, entirely met the increase of costs of private education. After Lombardy's example, this policy has been subsequently introduced in some other regions in Italy.

### 1.2.2. Health

In Lombardy, the public role in health provision has been radically transformed over the last twelve years from that of a classic monopoly

**Table 1.1**   Lombard Region School Subsidies

|  | Applications | % Accepted | Beneficiaries (no. of students) | Beneficiaries (no. of families) | Total Budget |
|---|---|---|---|---|---|
| 2001 | 55,040 | 85.83% | 47,241 | 47,241 | €30,740,742 |
| 2002 | 51,131 | 94.83% | 57,527 | 48,489 | €36,012,743 |
| 2003 | 51,200 | 94.34% | 57,914 | 48,300 | €37,024,750 |
| 2004 | 52,907 | 96.11% | 61,404 | 50,851 | €40,092,605 |
| 2005 | 54,141 | 95.88% | 63,044 | 51,912 | €42,054,000 |
| 2006 | 55,678 | 96.11% | 64,805 | 53,514 | €43,889,544 |
| 2007 | 57,847 | 92.25% | 65,411 | 53,364 | €45,123,437 |

Since 2008, this measure has become part of a broader set of interventions (*"dote scuola"*) targeted to the students of both public and private schools.

|  | Applications | % Accepted | Beneficiaries (no. of students) | Beneficiaries (no. of families) | Total Budget |
|---|---|---|---|---|---|
| 2008 | 61,501 | 99.39% | 61,130 |  | €44,832,904 |
| 2009 |  |  | 64,806 |  | €48,418,133 |
| 2010 |  |  | 67,000 (provisional) |  |  |

*Source*: The author's own elaboration on the basis of Lombard region, Dept. of Education and Professional Training Datas, 2010.

service provider, to one of strategy, regulation of provision, and finance.

Once recognized by the region on the basis of well-defined rules and standards of quality, nonstate providers are refunded for the services provided to customers who, for their part, are free to choose between state and private services for their needs, as they are charged with the same fees. Quality-dependent tariffs, a single regional card for social and health services, and the waiting-time targets provide further incentives (Balduzzi, 2005).

The resulting competition among health service providers should raise the quality, variety, and efficiency across the health sector. As a matter of fact, the high standards of Lombard health services and structures have been acknowledged by several independent evaluations, and indeed are the main motives driving thousands of Italians from other regions to take advantage of them. The flow of patients from other regions coming to Lombardy for health treatment has significantly increased by 35 percent (IReR, 2005, p. 416). At present the percentage of patients coming from other regions amounts to 10 percent (20 percent of total Italian patients) with peaks of 50 percent in some specialized areas such as cardiovascular and oncology treatments.

Further means for the achievement of excellence and integration have been introduced, such as specific tariff mechanisms rewarding virtuous structures that respond to the public's demands and punishing those less efficient.

### 1.2.3. Freedom of Choice

Finally, the inspiration of subsidiarity is also apparent in the reforms of other welfare services in Lombardy, in areas ranging from the labor market to the family. In the personal care for elderly and disabled people, for instance, a system of vouchers has been established to enable every family to bear the costs of caregiving to persons in need, or to choose among public and private service providers when specific professional assistance is needed. As for the health sector, this system—recently put into practice—is likely to enhance the quality and quantity of services offered in the near future in Lombard territory, though at the moment most services of this kind are still provided by local authorities.

Some indicators signal positive results for the efforts undertaken thus far to enhance citizens' responsibility and reduce levels of dependency. Admissions to hospitals have fallen by 15 percent from 1995 to

2003, while day-hospital care has risen by 73 percent, and the average staying of patients in hospital has been reduced by 18 percent (from 10 to 8.5 days). Residences for elderly people have also increased (from 436 in 1995 to 571 in 2004) but this is due to fact that CDI (*Centri diurni integrati*), centers for daily social and health care of elderly people which do not provide overnight stay service have been taken into account (CDIs have increased from 54 in 1995 to 121 in 2004) (IReR, 2005, p. 414).

## 1.3. The "Lombardy Model" and its Urgent Criticalities

Lombardy's governance experiment has been characterized by a distinctive, strong moral/ideological perspective, which differentiates it from outwardly similar policy reform efforts dominated by a technocratic focus on public service efficiency. A number of challenges remain, and they emerge as recurrent themes in several contributions to this volume.

If public resources are to be used in the service of civil society (rather than directly in the monopoly provision of services to citizens), there will need to be a transparent and effective auditing framework, robust to the classical risks (including a bias for the measurable over the relevant, and to distorted behavioral responses to targets).

Entrenched organized special interests and bureaucratic inertia imply significant path dependency in social policy (see Le Grand, 2007 for the health sector specifically).

In a subsidiarity-inspired model of social service provision, cost control can no longer be achieved by rationing and national pay-setting. In the absence of a valid alternative, financial pressures and crises can result (as indeed they have in recent British events, above all the near collapse—at the time of writing—of the largest single provider of residential care services, Southern Cross), as well as more insidious inequalities—whether driven by income, patient knowledge and articulacy, or post code.

If finance is "the spinal cord of devolution" (Bogdanor, 2001), it must follow that a full application of the principle of subsidiarity requires "that the political system promote the Third sector with legislative and fiscal rules and measures" (Donati, 2005, p. 76), because "the freedom of choice must be supported by a system of fiscal subsidiarity that allow to waive taxes on donations and contributions to the Third sector" (Maccarini, 2005, p. 135).

The Lombard model stands apart not only from the traditional Italian welfare system, but also from the fundamentally pragmatic or even technocratic approaches to public services reforms pursued elsewhere. This ideological distinctiveness seems analytically central to a correct interpretation of its regional governance, and to the thrust of future policy initiatives, which are likely to differ significantly from those derived from merely technocratic or neoliberal agendas.

## REFERENCES

Althusius, J. (1603) *Politica metodice digesta.* http://www.constitution.org/alth/alth_09.htm, accessed on September 23, 2011. Aquinas, T. (1946) "Summa theologiae" in *Scritti politici* [Political Writings] (Milano: Zanichelli)—my translation.

Aristotle, *Politics, Book One.* http://www.perseus.tufts.edu/cgibin/ptext?d oc=Perseus%3Atext%3A1999.01.0058&query=book%3D%231, accessed on September 23, 2011.

Balduzzi, R. (2005) "La legislazione sanitaria: il modello lombardo" in IReR, *Lombardia 2005. Società, governo e sviluppo del sistema Lombardo. Dieci anni di esperienze. Area istituzionale* (Milan: Guerini), 133–37.

Barber, N. W. (2005) "The limited modesty of subsidiarity" in *European Law Journal*, 11(3), 308–25.

Bogdanor, V. (2001) *Devolution in the United Kingdom* (Oxford: Oxford University Press).

Carlen, C. (ed.) (1990) *The Papal Encyclicals* (5 vols.) (Ann Arbor: Pierian). Carozza, P. (2003) "Subsidiarity as a structural principle of international human rights law" in *American Journal of International Law*, 97, 38–79.

Colombo, A. (2008) "The 'Lombardy Model': Subsidiarity-informed regional governance" in *Social Policy & Administration*, 42(2), 177–96.

Colombo, A., and S. Zaninelli (1998) "Stato e formazioni sociali nell'Italia repubblicana. Storia di una competenza negata" in G. Vittadini (ed.), *Sussidiarietà, la riforma possibile* (Milan: Etas), 5–39.

De Carli, P. (2005) "Famiglia, assistenza sociale e scolastica nelle due ultime legislature della regione Lombardia" in IReR (2005) *Lombardia 2005. Società, governo e sviluppo del sistema Lombardo. Dieci anni di esperienze. Area istituzionale* (Milan: Guerini), 121–31.

de Tocqueville, A. (1954) *Democracy in America* (New York: Vintage Books). Donati, P. (2005) "La sussidiarietà come forma di governance societaria in un mondo in via di globalizzazione" in P. Donati and I. Colozzi (eds.), *La sussidiarietà. Che cos'è e come funziona* (Rome: Carocci), 53–87.

Donati, P. (2007) "Sussidiarietà e nuovo welfare: oltre la concezione Hobbesiana del Benessere" in G. Vittadini (ed.), *Che cosa è la sussidiarietà. Un altro nome della libertà* (Milan: Guerini), 27–50.

Duret, P. (2000) "La 'sussidiarietà orizzontale': Le radici e le suggestioni di un concetto" in *JUS*, 95.

Follesdal, A. (2000) "Subsidiarity and democratic deliberation" in E. O. Eriksen and J. E. Fossum (eds.), *Democracy and the European Union: Integration Through Deliberation* (London: Routledge), 85–105.

Hoffmann, R. (1993) "Il principio di sussidiarietà. L'attuale significato nel diritto costituzionale Tedesco ed il possible ruolo nell'ordinamento dell'Unione europea" in *Rivista italiana di diritto pubblico comunitario*, 3, 23–41.

IReR (2005) *Lombardia 2005. Società, governo e sviluppo del sistema Lombardo. Dieci anni di esperienze* (Milan: Guerini).

Le Grand, J. (2007) "Sustaining responsibility: Quasi-markets and baby bonds" in IReR *The Lombardy Way* series of seminars (June) Available at: http://www.irer.it/eventi/governancerelazionigiugno2007/Le%20 Grand.pdf.

Locke, J. (1956) *The Second Treatise of Government* (Oxford: Blackwell).

Maccarini, M. E. (2005) "I modelli di attuazione della sussidiarietà orizzontale" in P. Donati and I. Colozzi (eds.), *La Sussidiarietà. Che cos'è e come funziona* (Rome: Carocci), 113–35.

Mill, J. S. (1903) *On Liberty* (London: Watts).Mulcahy, R. E. (1967) *Subsidiarity. In New Catholic Encyclopedia*, 13, 761–63.

Poggi, G. (1990) *The State: Its Nature, Development, and Prospects* (Stanford, CA: Stanford University Press).

Rinella, A. (1999) "Il principio di sussidiarietà: definizioni, comparazioni e modello d'analisi" in A. Rinella, L. Coen and R. Scarmiglia (eds.), *Sussidiarietà e ordinamenti costituzionali. Esperienze a confronto* (Padova: Cedam).

# 2

# Subsidiarity and the New Governance: Reflections on the Lombard Experience

## Lester M. Salamon

## 2.1. Introduction

This brief report is intended to offer a preliminary assessment of the model of governance developed in the Lombard region of Italy during the past fifteen years.[1] More specifically, the report focuses on the extent to which this model has served its avowed goal of advancing an approach to governance embodied in the concept of subsidiarity (Colombo and Mazzoleni, 2007). To do so, his report proceeds in three steps. First, it identifies a number of distinguishing features of the "Lombardy model" of public problem-solving that became at least partially apparent in the course of this preliminary review. Second, it calls attention to several potential tensions in what turn out to be three somewhat different conceptual impulses underlying the Lombard approach. Finally, it outlines a series of features that a true "subsidiarity-inspired" model of governance could be expected to exhibit, and preliminarily assesses the extent to which they seem to be present in the Lombard case.

## 2.2. Distinguishing Features of the Lombard Model

Even the most casual observer of the Lombard model of public problem-solving over the past fifteen years cannot help but be impressed by the extent of innovation that is on display there. The dimensions of this innovation are multiple, moreover.

### 2.2.1. New Concepts

In the first place, a major feature distinguishing the Lombard approach to addressing public problems is its conceptual coherence. The government of Lombardy has embraced a long-standing concept of Catholic social doctrine around which to build its governing philosophy, though it has adapted this concept in ways that its originator might not easily recognize. The concept in question is the doctrine of subsidiarity first enunciated by Pope Pius IX in his 1931 encyclical *Quadragesimo Anno*. Pius used the term "subsidiarity" to urge a policy of restraint on the part of governmental authorities and a preference for reliance on "subordinate groups" to handle "matters of lesser importance" than those "that belong to [the state] alone because it alone can do them."

In the hands of Lombard authorities, the lexicon of subsidiarity has been deployed to move from a state-centered to a society-centered approach to policy problems. The centerpiece of this approach is a concerted effort to engage a wide variety of social actors in addressing societal problems. This approach goes well beyond the neoliberal ideology that has inspired much of the recent government-reform efforts throughout the world. In particular, while seeking to engage social actors other than the state, it is not antistate. Rather, it promotes a new role for the state, one that acknowledges explicitly the need for a collaborative approach to solving public problems. As such, it bears strong resemblance to what I have termed "the new governance," an approach that emphasizes the collaborative nature of modern public problem-solving and the proliferation of new tools of public action such as contracting-out and vouchers through which such collaborations are built. Far from eliminating the state, however, the new governance framework emphasizes the need for a different kind of state and a different type of public management, one that relies on networks rather than hierarchical agencies, that emphasizes public-private cooperation, and that consequently requires new negotiation and persuasion skills rather than the command and control apparatus of traditional public administration (Salamon, 2002, pp. 1–46).

### 2.2.2. New Institutions

Accompanying the articulation of a new concept of public action has been the promotion of new institutions through which to address public problems. This institutional innovation has been driven by a commitment to ensuring "pluralism of offer," that is, an array of institutional choices for the consumers of publicly funded services.

This has meant the deconstruction of public action by separating the financing of services from their delivery, and increased reliance on both already-existing and new nonpublic institutions to deliver publicly financed services.

Among the notable developments here has been an explicit policy of encouraging social cooperatives, a new institutional form blending elements of for-profit business with features characteristic of public-benefit associations. Over 1,500 such cooperatives now operate in Lombardy. About 60 percent are so-called Type A social cooperatives providing a variety of welfare-type services to the elderly and to special-needs populations. The remainder are Type B social cooperatives that are distinguished not by the type of service they offer, but by the fact that at least 30 percent of their workers must be marginalized or disadvantaged individuals for whom the social cooperative's "business" is part of their road to self-sufficiency.

Another manifestation of the commitment to new institutional structures has been the major reconstruction of the health sector with the separation of the management functions and service delivery functions of former public hospitals, the creation of so-called *Aziende Sanitarie Locali* (ASLs), and the encouragement of private hospitals, both for-profit and nonprofit.

### 2.2.3. New Choices

A third feature of the Lombard model is its endorsement of consumer choice in the provision of publicly financed services. This is, of course, the other side of the coin of institutional innovation. Lombard policymakers have replaced producer-side subsidies with consumer-side subsidies in a wide variety of areas. Thus, they have created school vouchers (*buono scuola*) for vocational education, a family fund to finance a wide array of social services, a "social health-care voucher" for health services, and are experimenting with individual endowments (*doti*) for long-term human capital development.

### 2.2.4. New Citizen Engagement

A fourth notable feature of the Lombard model is its promotion of citizen engagement in the policy process. Perhaps the most notable illustration of this is the "family association" initiative launched by the Ministry of Social Affairs to engage groups of families to come together to help address community problems.

Approximately seven hundred such associations have been formed and the region devotes €8 million per year to supporting them.

## 2.3. Tensions in the Lombard Model

While the Lombard model thus displays an unusual degree of conceptual clarity and coherence, it also manifests some significant internal tension. This tension results from the fact that while the model is inspired by the concept of subsidiarity, the actual measures taken to implement this concept have been inspired by another strategic concept, namely the concept of quasi markets.

Further complicating things, the concept of subsidiarity itself has two distinct components—one vertical and the other horizontal. The result is not a single integrated conceptual basis for policy decisions, but a troika that policy leaders have assumed will always pull in the same direction, but in practice often does not. A brief look at these three impulses will illustrate the tensions at work.

### 2.3.1. Vertical Subsidiarity

While the religious doctrine of subsidiarity focuses on horizontal relationships between government and other societal institutions, such as associations, there is also a more secular version of the concept that focuses instead on vertical relationships between higher governmental authorities and lower ones.

Subsidiarity in this sense is thus another term for federalism, for the preservation of a meaningful degree of autonomy for lower levels of government.

This dimension of subsidiarity has figured prominently in debates over European integration, as nation-states have struggled to preserve important components of national sovereignty in the face of the growing power of far-off European institutions.

As a regional government in a traditionally unitary Italian nation-state, it is understandable why the government of Lombardy would embrace the concept of subsidiarity in its vertical sense. This concept provides a religiously sanctioned justification for Lombardy's drive for institutional autonomy within the Italian nation. This has not only philosophical but also more concrete implications. The Lombard region is a net contributor of resources to the Italian nation: it gives more in tax revenues than it receives back in the form of national subsidies, services, and investments. Subsidiarity provides a rationale for keeping more of these resources at home and for getting out from under the central government's control.

This is not to say that subsidiary in its vertical dimensions has no broader substantive rationale. Rather, the decentralization that subsidiary promotes can be an important stimulus to innovation. Decentralized structures foster experimentation by freeing local units from the often-deadening hand of highly centralized bureaucratic structures.

Counterbalancing this, however, is the harsh reality that excessive decentralization and autonomy can work against the promotion of equity and basic rights. This is certainly the experience in the United States, where the slogan of "states rights," another term for vertical subsidiarity, became a code word for denial of basic rights of citizenship for millions of African American citizens and for continued gross disparities in the provision of basic health, education, and welfare services among US states. While good for Lombardy, vertical subsidiarity may thus not be good for Italy as a whole, or at least not necessarily and entirely so.

## 2.3.2. Horizontal Subsidiarity

Quite apart from its vertical dimension and much more in line with its original religious roots, subsidiarity also has a significant horizontal dimension. In fact, it is this dimension that really distinguishes the Lombard model of governance in conceptual terms, as noted above. Horizontal subsidiarity refers to the relationship between government and society and it promotes active governmental reliance on nonstate social actors.

While horizontal subsidiarity urges a society-centered approach to addressing public problems, however, it is not agnostic about which societal institutions to rely on. Rather, subsidiarity as a concept puts a premium on supporting institutions that engage people directly, that encourage solidarity, and promote self-help. These are typically associations and various cooperative-type institutions. Such institutions are viewed from this perspective not only as producers of services, but also as generators of "relational capital," those bonds of trust and reciprocity that are thought to be ultimately critical for the operation of a market system and the flourishing of democracy. As Brugnoli and Vittadini (2009, p. 19) put it:

> Subsidiarity suggests [ ... ] that there is a need to see, to hear, to increase in value that which exists originally and freely develops "from

the bottom" as a response to the needs of individuals and the collec-
tivity [ ... ] The principle is based on the hypothesis that the person,
individually and in association with other persons, is potentially able
to confront collective needs and to satisfy them.

### 2.3.3. Quasi Markets

The third horse in the troika of impulses propelling the Lombard
model is the concept of quasi markets. Indeed, while the Lombard
model has been inspired by the concept of subsidiarity, most of the
policy initiatives through which it has been implemented have been
shaped by the concept of quasi markets. Fortunately, these two concepts share many common features. However, they are also not quite
identical.

The quasi-market concept calls for the introduction of market-type
relationships into the provision of publicly funded services (Bartlett
and LeGrand, 1993). To achieve this, the quasi-market approach promotes three basic changes in traditional publicly provided services:
first, the separation of the financing of services from their provision;
second, the replacement of "producer-side subsidies," that is, subsidies made available to the providers of services, with "consumer-
side subsidies," that is, those provided directly to users; and third,
the encouragement of open competition among providers for the
"business" of consumers and the creation of circumstances that per-
mit users to make informed choices. Essentially, the quasi-market
approach thus seeks to break the public-sector monopoly on the provision of public services by creating at least a "quasi" market, all in
the hope of reducing costs and fostering responsiveness to user needs
and demands.

Clearly, with its emphasis on choice and empowerment of users,
as well as its hostility to public-sector monopolies, the quasi-market
approach offers a promising vehicle through which to promote subsidiarity goals. At the same time, however, certain features of the
quasi-market approach create pressures that diverge from subsidiarity
principles, often sharply, even if unintentionally.

In the first place, while emphasizing the need for a "plurality" of
providers in order to ensure competition, the quasi-market approach
is generally agnostic about the nature of the providers that come
into the market: they can be for-profit, nonprofit, or public. The one
requirement is that they pass certain accreditation criteria. Beyond
this, quasi markets accepts all comers.

While this seems eminently fair, it overlooks the unlevel playing field that confronts nonprofit organizations in competing with for-profit firms. This results from certain inherent structural limitations of the nonprofit form. In particular, because they cannot distribute profits to owners or "shareholders," nonprofit organizations lack access to the equity markets: they cannot issue stock to raise capital for new facilities, equipment, or even soft-capital items such as strategic plans and staff development. This can become a critical impediment when governments open the spigot to pour substantial resources into the hands of consumers in particular fields and simultaneously impose new accreditation standards on suppliers. At such times, the organizations able to meet the new demand in the open market will expand their market share. But this often requires new facilities, new equipment, and newly trained staff—all of which requires capital, precisely the resource that nonprofits are structurally ill-equipped to generate. As a consequence, unless positive action is taken to offset this structural disadvantage of nonprofit providers, quasi markets can lead to the displacement of nonprofit providers, precisely the opposite of what subsidiarity seeks to accomplish.

This scenario has, in fact, played itself out in several fields in the United States as government has moved from producer-side subsidies such as grants and contracts to consumer-side subsidies such as vouchers and tax expenditures. For example, Medicare, America's health-insurance voucher program for the elderly, made home health care eligible for reimbursement for the first time in 1980 in an effort to lower health-care costs by moving patients out of high-cost hospital settings earlier. At the time, home health was a 70–80 percent nonprofit "business." Nonprofits had pioneered home health services and clearly dominated the (relatively small) market. But when home health became eligible for Medicare reimbursement, a rush of resources flooded the market. Seeing an opportunity, for-profit health-care companies moved quickly to take advantage of the bonanza, floating initial public offerings of stock to generate capital, building new facilities, and thereby transforming the field. Within five to eight years what had been a nonprofit-dominated field had become a for-profit dominated field, with nonprofits falling to below 30 percent of the facilities. This same experience has been replicated in other fields as well, such as psychiatric hospitals and kidney dialysis centers (Salamon, 2004, p. 19).

From the preliminary evidence at hand, something similar now seems to be happening in Lombardy, at least in the health sector. For-profit hospitals seem to be gaining ground and nonprofit and public ones losing ground in this field, as the dynamics of the market work their will on the structure of this market.

To date, there is little evidence that for-profits are penetrating the social-care market, but this may be because the reimbursement rates in this field are too low to attract for-profit competitors. But such reimbursement rates can limit the ability of the nonprofit providers to offer the service quality that is needed or to perform the other social functions ascribed to them by the subsidiarity concept.

This brings us to a second divergence between quasi markets and subsidiarity. Quasi markets emphasize a particular role for the recipients of publicly financed services: the role of consumer. While diverging from neoliberalism by recognizing a continuing important role for government, the quasi-market concept nevertheless embraces the neoliberal idea that market relationships provide the proper template for the structuring of public services. The governing analogy of quasi markets is that of the individual consumer exercising freedom of choice in a competitive market for service. This diverges sharply, however, from the emphasis in subsidiarity on a quite different social role for individuals: the role of citizen, of participant in a joint process of promoting the common good.

What is more, the subsidiarity concept, as noted, conceives of a different role for nonprofit associations: they are not simply producers of services equivalent to any other contributor to the "pluralism of offer" (Brugnoli and Vittadini, 2009, p. 28). Rather, they are perceived to have a much broader social function as promoters of social solidarity, as vehicles through which individuals can join together to achieve socially desirable goals, and as mechanisms for encouraging citizen participation in public decisions.

The attenuation of the citizen role that can result from the quasi-market approach can take an even more dangerous form if not actively combated. Quasi markets, indeed collaborative government more generally, can inadvertently lead to a deterioration of a sense of community. It can do so by breaking the visible link between the taxes people pay and the services they receive. This can happen when the taxes go to the state but the services come from private, nonprofit, or for-profit agencies. Over time, citizens can lose track of the real source of the aid they are receiving and turn even further against the taxes that support the services they receive. The recent debate over health care in the United States offers a chilling reminder of these dangers as numerous elderly residents raised alarms about a proposed "public" health insurance option on grounds that it might undermine Medicare, not realizing that Medicare is itself a "public" health insurance program.

## 2.4. PRESERVING SUBSIDIARITY IN A QUASI-MARKET ENVIRONMENT: WHAT CAN BE DONE?

While there are tensions between the quasi-market and subsidiarity approaches, however, there are also ways to reduce them. But this requires positive actions and concerted strategies. Fortunately, the government of Lombardy has put in place a number of such actions but it does not yet seem to have formulated a clear strategy that takes account of the tensions between these two strands of its model and designed steps to reduce them. The following seven steps provide a sort of template for such a strategy and a scorecard for gauging how far the region has put such a strategy into place.

1. *Government must view the public and the users of its services as "citizens" and not just "consumers" of services.*

   In practice this requires reasonable efforts to engage citizens in deliberations over the content of service offerings, participation in their delivery, and the assessment of their results. To the extent possible, this should be done with the participation of the third-sector organizations offering services so that they retain a significant community organizing and relationship-building role. The promotion of "family associations" by the Ministry of Social Welfare provides a useful example of an active engagement strategy, though it was not clear whether the ministry engaged the civil society organizations in helping to form and manage these associations.

2. *Government must view third-sector organizations as partners, not simply contract service providers.*

   This requires regular communication with third-sector service providers about contract administration and program content. It also means encouragement of programmatic innovation by providers and a willingness to be flexible in allowing such innovations to proceed. Innovation funds, innovation award programs, and the like can contribute to this.

3. *Government must involve civil society organizations in the design, not merely the delivery, of government-funded programs.*

   Third-sector organizations involved in delivering publicly funded services are an important fount of knowledge about the problems citizens are encountering and the adequacy of programs designed to address them. This knowledge should be actively tapped in the design and in the reengineering of public programs. Regular forums for discussion and debate about program content and administrative operations would help contribute to this result, as would clearly articulated principles that both government and third-sector organizations agree to abide by to guide their relationship. Some countries (e.g., the UK) have negotiated "compacts" between third-sector organizations and the government to crystallize these operating principles and make sure government officials and third-sector leaders are aware of them.

4. *Government must invest in civil society organizations capacity.*

   As the subsidiarity principle calls for government to rely heavily on civil society organizations to deliver publicly funded services, government has a deep stake in the capacity of these organizations, since government's own record of accomplishment will depend on this capacity. Establishing accreditation standards may be one way to promote improved capacity, but in the absence of sufficient capacity-building resources such standards can end up forcing nonprofits from the field rather than equipping them to perform better in it. Just as government invests in the training of its own personnel, so, too, must it invest in the capacities of the entities that are increasingly delivering its services. This implies support for staff development, strategic planning, improved technology, and administrative improvement.

5. *Government should take steps to offset the capital constraint facing civil society organizations.*

   Of particular concern to the viability of a subsidiarity impulse in the context of a quasi-market policy agenda is the ability of nonprofits to secure the capital that they need to remain competitive. Government should recognize its responsibility to preserve at least the rudiments of a level playing field so far as access to capital by third-sector associations is concerned. This can be done in any of a number of ways—for example, by offering loan guarantees that reduce the cost of private loan capital for associations, by creating tax incentives for the purchase of government bonds used to underwrite the cost of facilities and equipment needed for associations, by providing direct grants or low-interest loans to upgrade civil society organization facilities and equipment.

6. *Government should allow for full cost recovery for civil society organizations, including indirect costs and costs for mission-critical functions.*

   Governments frequently allow a profit margin in their reimbursement systems for for-profit organizations but not for nonprofit ones. However, associations perform important functions beyond those involved in the delivery of publicly funded services. These include advocacy work, community organizing, and generally promoting solidarity. What is more, in addition to costs that can easily be identified with particular services there are also "indirect costs" that cannot easily be attributed to particular activities. These include general administrative costs, the costs of utilities and facilities, proposal and fundraising costs, and the like. Care should be taken in the setting of reimbursement rates to make provision for at least some of these mission-critical functions. Reimbursement arrangements that focus exclusively on minimizing the unit cost of services will drive out precisely those qualities that make third-sector organizations desirable partners for government in the first place, particularly if these arrangements are combined with accreditation requirements that utilize rigid design standards (e.g., percentages of personnel with particular credentials) instead of more flexible performance standards (e.g., a record of success in achieving program outcomes).

7. *Government should monitor the evolution of the institutional structure.*

A government that is serious about promoting subsidiarity while implementing quasi-market policies should pay attention to the institutional structure that is resulting, whether intentionally or unintentionally, from its policy innovations. Of particular concern, of course, is the impact of these policies on associations and other third-sector organizations. This will require the conduct of "focus groups" with such organizations and the collection of periodic data on the growth or decline of their employment, their fiscal health, and the relative position of not-for-profit and for-profit establishments. From the evidence at hand, it appears that data are being collected on at least one set of such organizations—the social cooperatives—but not of third-sector organizations more generally. In the absence of such information, it will be hard to formulate meaningful strategies to ensure that the subsidiarity objectives are really being achieved.

## 2.5. CONCLUSIONS

The government of Lombardy has distinguished itself among regional and national authorities by the clarity and distinctiveness of its governing philosophy and objectives. The principle of subsidiarity that it has embraced usefully acknowledges a fundamental reality about modern public problem-solving, a reality stressed as well in the "new governance" conception generated in the United States: that contemporary problems are too complex to be solved by any one sector, that government must find ways to enlist the creativity and energy of other sectors, and that this will require important changes in how government itself operates, but changes that involve more complex tasks and skills not a surrender of governmental responsibilities.

Putting these principles to work is no easy task and the government of Lombardy has made enormous strides in this direction. At the same time, its actions to date have exposed some tensions between two of the three conceptual impulses that have formed the foundation of its innovations—subsidiarity and quasi markets. The next phase of development of this intriguing model might well be to take the steps needed to reduce these tensions. Hopefully, the ideas outlined here, emphasizing the need for a more coherent and proactive partnership between the regional authorities and civil society organizations can provide useful markers on how this could be done.

## NOTE

1. I am indebted to Roberta Bonini of Éupolis Lombardia for arranging these interviews and to Elisa Di Napoli and Monica Bergo for facilitating a fruitful exchange of concepts and understandings.

## REFERENCES

Bartlett, W. and J. Le Grand (1993) *Quasi-markets and Social Policy* (London: Palgrave Macmillan).

Brugnoli, A., and G. Vittadini (2009) *Subsidiarity: Positive Anthropology and Social Organization. Foundations for a New Conception of State and Market and Key Points of the Experience in Lombardy* (Milan: Guerini).

Colombo, A., and M. Mazzoleni (2007) *Lombardy's Model of Governance: Empowering Communities and Society with the Freedom to Grow* (Milan: IReR Working Paper).

Salamon, L. M. (2002) "Introduction: The new governance and the tools of public action" in L. M. Salamon (ed.), *The Tools of Government: A Guide to the New Governance* (New York: Oxford University Press), 1–46.

Salamon, L. M. (2004) *The Resilient Sector: The State of Nonprofit America* (Washington, DC: Brookings Institution Press).

# 3

# A Hornet's Nest or the Climax of the Change of Regime? The Dilemmas of Creating Regions in Eastern and Central Europe

*Gyula Horváth*

## 3.1. Introduction

Regionalism, the regional decentralization of power and the distribution of labour among the different forms of local government, have found themselves in the crossfire of debate in the unitary states of Eastern and Central Europe. The change of the political system, the process of connecting to the globalizing European economy, the construction of a local governmental structure using the concepts of civic democracy, all shed new light on the mutual connections of central and regional local power, the harmonization of settlement independence and meso-level public administration functions (Horváth, 1996). In almost all of the former socialist countries the central issue has become that of the economic, political, and functional transformation of the basic levels of local government. The earlier subnational levels disappeared (as in the successor states of the old Czechoslovakia), their functions to a large extent decreased (as in Hungary), changed (as in Poland), or, alternatively, new regional meso-levels were created (as in Croatia) or are being created (as in Slovenia) (Blažek and Boeckhout, 2000; Illner, 2000; Szreniawski 2004; Tariska 2004).

The construction of regions in the countries of Eastern and Central Europe became one of the important debate topics for preparation for EU membership (Bachtler, Downes, and Gorzelak, 2000). However, the application of EU structural policy relates to appropriate size in terms of the population potential of subnational development units and their economic capacities, in view of the concepts of economies of scale, and so, during the preparation of the EU pre-accession programs, planning-statistical regions had to be created in all countries. From a formal point of view, solving this task did not create any particular problem. The government of each country listed the regional public administration units as meso-level development regions, and, on the basis of EU recommendations, the formal organizational structures (regional development councils, development directorates, and agencies) were also created.

In parallel with the creation of the organizational framework of an EU-compatible development policy, there started, in most countries, an intensive debate on issues of content. In these debates, numerous issues (which had earlier received less attention among the topics relating to the change of regime) were raised: What functions should the development regions have? How can they become public administration units serving the decentralization of the centralized state system? What resources should they have to fulfill the development programs? Which city in the region should become the regional center?

EU accession opened up a pandora's box in the countries of Eastern and Central Europe. The fundamental issue of how unitarily structured states can be set on a decentralized path became the center of debate. This present study searches for an explanation of the reasons for the difficulties of Eastern and Central Europe in regional construction; it summarizes the administrative and political development prerequisites of the transition to a regional outline of the possible advantages of a regional institutional system in the creation of the Cohesion policy ensuring a decrease in regional differences.

## 3.2. THE FORMAL CHANGE IN REGIONAL ADMINISTRATION

The new nation-states in Eastern and Central Europe established in the aftermath of World War I had to face—from the point of view of their future regional development—two difficulties. One of the issues to be addressed was how to create a unified structure for those (new) parts of the country that earlier had been developed in different economic areas, in order to link their infrastructure systems. The other was to create a new system of regional organization of central government power. The heavily centralized state powers created their own regional bodies partly on their former administration basis, but completing those tasks needed to create the new, unified state territory that was most effectively assisted by the low number of administrative units involved. Following World War II, the Soviet-style regional administration was organized differently—now based upon different power considerations. The Communist states, in accordance with their political interests, heavily changed the countries' regional administration on several occasions, sometimes organizing smaller regional units and sometimes larger. Hungary can be considered as an exception to this, in that, in the twentieth century (apart from some underpopulated counties being combined) the number of subnational units in the country has not changed (see Table 3.1).

In Eastern and Central Europe a hierarchical planning organizational system—with a fairly powerful central planning office at the top in each country—had previously been the decisive organizational form of regional development. Regional development based on central large scale investment and state social policy did not require a multiparticipant institutional system operating in horizontal cooperation. In addition, the state's interest in redistribution, together with the central will, were carried out most effectively by vertically subordinated organizations. This philosophy of state organization also defined the regional administration system.

Although public administration under socialism did not differ significantly from that of the developed democracies in respect of form and certain operational concepts, it produced an unusual administrative organization—despite the dominant organizational concept of the (so called) "democratic centralism" and the omnipotence of the Communist Party. The local organs of power to a very large extent (and especially in the first three decades of extensive industrialization

**Table 3.1**   Changes in the Number of Regional Administrative Units in Eastern and Central European Countries

| Country | Pre-World War II | 1950s | 1960s | 1970s | 1980s | 2005 |
|---|---|---|---|---|---|---|
| Bulgaria | 9 | 13 | 28 | 28 | 9 | 28[1999] |
| Czech Republic | 2 | 13 | 8 | 8 | 8 | 14[2001] |
| Hungary | 25 | 20 | 20 | 20 | 20 | 20 |
| Poland | 14 | 22 | 22 | 49 | 49 | 16[1999] |
| Romania | 9 | 18 | 18 | 40 | 41 | 42 |
| Slovakia | 2 | 6 | 4 | 4 | 4 | 8[1996] |

*Source*: The author's own chart, 2010.

and settlement development) imposed the central will by diktat, ignoring any kind of potential advantage that a region might have in development terms. However, as the strongly centralized state system in countries such as Poland and Hungary gradually softened, local initiatives were given greater opportunities, and, due to this, in these countries in the 1980s, civic values in respect of settlement development—such as improvements in services and private house construction—made their appearance.

Following the change of regime, the organizational framework of Eastern and Central European states underwent important conceptual changes. A local government structure has replaced the hierarchical, executive council system, and the related legislation has created the constitutional basis for a decentralized exercise of power. By now, in fact, local authorities have been equipped with constitutional guarantees of their organizational and decision-making independence, and very significant changes have been introduced into local government financing. In formal terms, public administration in Romania and Hungary has remained unchanged, although in Bulgaria the previous multicounty system was restored. At the same time, both the Czech Republic and Slovakia (as in the period between 1949 and 1960) created counties relatively small in size. Only Poland established large size "*voivod*-ships" and here the reform of the country's public administration has been an important milestone in the process of preparing for EU Accession (Pálné, 2007).

The other country to be devoted to regionalization is Hungary. Hungarian meso-level units—if we look retrospectively over several centuries—partly because of their actual size and partly because of their greatly weakened positions after the change of regime (a counterreaction to the political role that they played in the planned economy) are simply not competent to undertake large-scale development tasks. In the twentieth century, several attempts to modernize public administration in this strongly uni-centered country were made, but, one after the other, all of the plans failed, due to their rejection by central government and due to a lack of agreement among the regional political elites. In 2006, the government—within the framework of the general reform of public administration—submitted a legislative program to Parliament for the reorganization of regional administration. The Parliamentary opposition, however, has not supported the legislative program (to amend the Hungarian Local Government Act, a two-thirds majority in Parliament is required, but the government coalition parties fall well short of this).

It is, therefore, quite evident that the question of the public administration units (meso-level) positioned between central government and the settlements will continue to be an open issue—and also extremely important from the point of view of regional policy. It is, in fact, a general phenomenon in Eastern and Central Europe that these levels—as a reaction to the negative role that they mainly played under the previous system and their extremely strong political and redistributive functions—have very few local administration rights.

In recent decades, important differences can be seen between Western and Eastern Europe in the operation of the regional administration system and its changes of function. In the EU member states—after the Single European Act was ratified—the role of the subnational level became more important—partly, since it resulted in the extension of the new general organizational concept of the European Communities—that is, subsidiarity, (following the amendment of the original concept). However, the level below that of central government was also handed a key role from the (Common European) Regional Policy point of view. The new structural and supportive policy laid down—as a basic concept—cooperation with the local regional authority (these having weak structures and deteriorating economies) and coordination between regional and national economic development strategies.

The realization of the market economy and the structural reorganization of the economy, relatively quickly made it clear that regional tensions cannot be reduced, regional political aims (as set out in most of the countries) cannot be fulfilled, and regional programs cannot be elaborated without a radical reform of the functions of the regional meso-levels. Consequently, it was no accident that the review of meso-level functions evoked in each country the issue of the institutionalization of regionalization, the creation of a low number of regional units—similar in size and armed with similar rights as the regional meso-levels in the West European regional and decentralized states.

The unitary states of Europe—consequent upon the globalization and internationalization of the economy and the increased sophistication of European integration—can relatively soon move toward a new order of state structure. The factors supporting the further development and rethinking of meso-level public administration in Eastern and Central Europe are as follows:

1. The phenomena of disintegration experienced in the local government sphere indicate that the links between legal and specific interest issues are lacking, with the consequence that the notion

of the model as working exclusively and voluntarily on a "bottom-up" basis seems to be both misleading and unrealistic;

2.  Due to the (basically, single-level) system of local government, regional development responsibilities are left uncontrolled, and attempts are made to plug this gap by the, now deconcentrated, state organs, with one part of the (deconcentrated) administration penetrating into the vacuum left at meso-level, but undertaking tasks foreign to the organization and with its segmented structure resulting in a hiatus in the process of coordination and information, as well as in the reconciliation of interests;

3.  The disintegration of local government and the dysfunction of deconcentrated public administration gave new life to central governmental trials, and in regional public administration units a model with state and local government in competition with each other began to appear;

4.  The tendency toward nationalization at meso-level is, of course, in direct opposition to the EU's integration process, but this contradiction can be resolved by the creation of a local government meso-level;

5.  An important future responsibility for regional public administration can be to represent and defend the concept of interregional cooperation against the organs of central government, and it should be remembered that "the Europe of the Regions"—as one of the key concepts of European integration—can be conceived of only with the cooperation of regional units of relatively similar competencies and complexity.

## 3.3. THE DEVELOPMENT PLANNING REGIONS

A prerequisite for Eastern and Central European countries to join the EU or to benefit from support from the Structural Funds was the creation of large regions (NUTS-Nomenclature of Territorial Units for Statistics 2 units): on this basis the most effective development concepts and the programs serving their realization, could best be drawn up. The 206 NUTS 2 regions established in the fifteen member states of the EU are very different from the point of view of their public law and administration situation—and their physical size and population numbers. Basically, we are looking at units nationally determined, in which, at the same time as the NUTS 2 system of each country should meet common requirements, they operate as statistical (calculating, analyzing, planning, programming, coordinating ) and developing (support policy, decentralizing) units. In the ten associated East European countries the number of meso-level administration units at the end of 1999 was 357, and it was clear that the EU's support policy could not supervise such a high number of regional units. In consequence, it became essential to create larger regional development and statistical units.

Defining boundaries within the NUTS system is, from the EU's point of view, an internal affair—which means that, apart from size, there are no absolute EU requirements in terms of the creation of the regions: the decision lies within the scope of national governments. However, on the basis of experience with creating regions, the various concepts and likely impacts can be expressed in a way that makes the definition of the region relatively straightforward:

1. a prehistory of regional cooperation and, hence, the chances of regional cohesion;
2. relative size status from the point of view of the national regional structure;
3. relative spatial homogeneity in terms of the basic aims of regional policy;
4. an effective internal structure (center, subcenters, skills, and the ability to cooperate etc.) of a region and the observance of public administration borders;
5. the existing (or demanded) "geo-political" similarity of the units united in a region and the degree of identity of the definitive, long-term, international orientations;
6. the costs of creating and operating the regions (decision preparing, decision making and professional administrative background institutions, organizing the information, planning, managing, and monitoring activities, the institutional system of decentralized financing, etc.), the economies of scale from a functional point of view;
7. the existence of a multifunctional, major urban regional center.

The NUTS 2 regions are listed in the Regional Development Acts or Government Decrees of each country. However, the Regional Development Act adopted in Hungary in 1996 was quite cautious, indicating merely that the counties could create regions in order to carry out common tasks. It did not, however, define the development regions of the country; and this imprecise regulation had, as a consequence, the fact that counties joined together widely differing regions purely for fund-raising purposes—and there were counties that participated in three or four regional alliances. However, the amendment to the act in 1999 defined seven development-statistical regions and separated the counties into regions. In fact, a Government Decree listing, in an itemized form, the theoretical concepts defining development regions was created only in Bulgaria (Geshev, 2001). The Bulgarian government defined the aspects of the creation of the regions in 1999 as follows:

1. The number of regions should be relatively low and they should be defined on the basis of their size and natural resource potential; their economic and social capacities should be able to undertake large-scale programs;
2. The regions should not be too large to be manageable, and the number of counties comprising a region should be optimal in order to be able to be organize their cooperation;
3. There should be a common development problem in the region, which could be felt in any point of the region and which motivates the regional development actors to cooperate;
4. Natural geographical units and historical traditions should be taken into consideration;
5. The region should have a relatively developed urban network and several growth-poles;
6. The planning region should comprise complete public administration units.

In the other countries, and after long debate, a compromise decision was reached in terms of the creation of NUTS 2 regions, and these (more or less) matched the above basic concepts. As regards size, they parallel very closely the average of the older EU member states (see Table 3.2). Individual countries, however, did not come to define their central regions in the same way. In Bulgaria, Poland, Hungary, and Romania, for example, the capitals, together with their surrounding "Greater" regions, made up one NUTS 2 unit, whilst, in the Czech Republic and Slovakia, the capitals alone constitute one single region. As it is visible in Eastern and Central Europe that general pattern of spatial economy in which the larger region surrounding a country's most developed growth pole can show weaker performance (a consequence of the "filtering-down" effect), this solution generated strong debate in Hungary. The overall performance of the Central Hungary Region (due to Budapest's high gross domestic product [GDP] per capita) is as much as 98 percent of the average of the EU-15 and cannot, therefore, be included in the target group for

**Table 3.2**   The Most Significant Data of NUTS 2 Units in Eastern and Central Europe

| Country | NUTS 2 Regions | | |
|---|---|---|---|
| | Number | Average Area ('000 km $^2$) | Average Population ('000s) |
| Bulgaria | 6 | 18.5 | 1,407 |
| Czech Republic | 8 | 9.9 | 1,290 |
| Hungary | 7 | 13.3 | 1,463 |
| Poland | 16 | 19.5 | 2,411 |
| Romania | 8 | 29.8 | 2,851 |
| Slovakia | 4 | 12.2 | 1,319 |
| Total | 49 | 14.7 | 1,910 |
| Total EU15 | 206 | 15.3 | 1,830 |

*Source*: The author's own calculations on the basis of Regions Statistical Yearbook 2004, 2010.

convergence. Support, therefore, will be more modest (Budapest itself produces 125 percent of the EU average, whilst the region's remaining unit, Pest County, produced just 53 percent in 2003). Similar problems can be noted in the other three countries also.

At the time when the development-statistical regions in Eastern and Central Europe were being laid out, those ethnocultural factors used in the organization of West European regions were not applied. In Romania, the three counties comprising the historical Székely territory were incorporated into the Central Region, in which half of the Hungarian population living in Romania (730,000 people) live. The three counties together could themselves have made up a separate development region with their population of 1.1 million people, but in this case the proportion of Hungarians in the population of the region would have been 59.2 percent. Romanian governmental pressures and political factors blocked the Székely territory from becoming an independent region, and a region with a population of 2.6 million was created—in which Hungarians make up less than one-third. The debates surrounding the creation of an individual Székely region have simply fuelled today's ethnic conflicts in Romania (Horváth, 2003).

In Slovakia, the neglect of ethnocultural factors was already detectable during the establishment of the new regional administrative system. The overwhelming majority of the Hungarian population live in the southern areas of the country bordering on Hungary. However, the borders of the new counties were drawn in such a way that large areas inhabited by Slovaks were attached to clusters of Hungarians, with the result that in none of the counties of Slovakia could the Hungarian population be the majority.

The organizational system of the development-statistical regions was introduced in each country on the basis of a scheme recommended by the European Union. Under this, development councils and development agencies operate in the regions, and these organizations are managed by the central regional development body. Their responsibilities are essentially restricted to simple coordination, to accumulating projects, and to assembling development plans. Their operative bodies, the development agencies, or directorates, work with from twenty to forty people, and their competency lies within a narrow framework. It can be seen as a general problem for member states that those favored under the programs were the central state administration bodies. In the central bodies of regional development, staff numbers were increased to several hundreds, whilst in the regions only a fraction of this number was possible. The weak position of the regions is also indicated by the fact that, in the programing period 2004–2006, only 17–30 percent of EU support was devoted to regional operative programs.

Since the regulations defining the composition of regions said nothing about regional centers (a task which, in any case, should not be handled within the framework of spatial development regulation) in most countries conflicts amongst cities and towns have broken out in individual regions for the privilege of becoming home to particular regional development institution.

## 3.4. IS EASTERN AND CENTRAL EUROPE UNITARY OR DECENTRALIZED?

Should it be thought desirable to give an important future role to the meso-level units in regional policy in Eastern and Central Europe, this would clearly bring the current meso-level system into sharp focus. Both the size and economic potential of the counties in their current form are too small for them to become the basic units of decentralized regional policy, and it is to be expected that, in the future, regionalism will become stronger in more and more countries, and that this will lend weight to the redefining of the distribution of labor between center and provinces. There will be a serious opportunity to establish interregional cooperation operating on the basis of economic conformity and to increase cohesion in Eastern and Central Europe—but, even then, only if the tasks now accumulating (a genuine regional decentralization of power and the creation of a regional development strategy conforming to the market economy) could be carried out, would it be possible that regionalism in its West European meaning could take root in this area. Today the driving forces of growth are concentrated in the core areas of individual countries, something that indicates, over the long term, the maintenance of the differences between the national regional units—or even their increase (see Table 3.3).

The changes occurring during the last decade indicate that the political scope of activity within regional policy at the beginning of the new century—over and above the self-determination of economic development—are defined by two major factors: the first of these is the EU's organizational, operational, and financial reform together with Eastern enlargement, whilst the second (to no small extent influenced by the first) is the establishment of a new distribution of labor within government in the nation-states—in other words, decentralization.

Decentralization—as proved most clearly by the processes of previous decades—is now regarded in Europe as a perfectly normal phenomenon. In 1950 a quarter of the population of the continent lived in federalized or regionalized states, a figure which, by the mid-90s had risen to 60 percent. By the end of the first decade of the following century—without taking into account the successor states of the former Soviet Union—more than three-quarters of the population of Europe will live in countries where influencing the factors of economic growth, it will not be the state but rather, the subnational level that will play the defining role. This quantitative change—according to our current knowledge—will be the result of the creation of new

**Table 3.3** The Weight of Capital Cities in Eastern and Central Europe, as Percentage of National Total, 2004

| Areas | Sofia [2002] | Prague | Budapest | Warsaw | Bratislava | Bucharest [2002] |
|---|---|---|---|---|---|---|
| GDP | 24.6 | 24.5 | 35.0 | n.a. | 24.2 | 16.5 |
| Industrial output | 15.9 | 13.0 | 17.6 | 11.8 | 37.3 | 17.0 |
| Foreign Capital Investment | 49.9 | 25.7 | 56.5 | 33.0 | 71.2 | 46.7 |
| University Student Numbers | 43.3 | 31.4 | 49.2 | 16.7 | 83.0 | 32.4 |
| R&D employees | 72.7 | 48.0 | 55.8 | 30.0 | 40.2 | 39.0 |

*Source*: Author's own construction based on National Statistical Yearbooks, 2010.

regional administration in two countries with a high population—the UK and Poland.

The basic interest of the nation-state in the future will be to try to use its power to determine economic policy within its borders to counterbalance the effects of external pressure from globalization and integration—by increasing the ability of the regions to defend their interests in a regulated fashion. It is already the case that the traditional regional development practice of Keynesian economic policy cannot be used successfully in the new paradigm, and the state's regional policy will be substituted by the region's own policy. This paradigm exchange, however, cannot occur automatically, the interests of the regions being developed to different levels. In the institutionalization of regionalism important differences are to be seen. The poorest regions can hope for improvement through outside (national and international) help, as in the past, their motivations depending more on traditional support systems than on what might be gained through the autonomy (in its wider sense) of a "Europe of the Regions." The devoted fans of regional decentralization come from the group of developed regions that will clearly be the beneficiaries of the single market and of the economic and monetary union. It is not by chance that, today, Europe's most efficient regional cooperation network (not even connected territorially) comprises: Baden-Württemberg, Lombardy, Rhône-Alpes, and Catalonia, who created a cooperation under the name "Europe's Four Engines" (Amin and Tomaney, 1995; Späth, 1989).

The general spread of regionalism, however, still faces large barriers, and national governments will continue in the future to play an important role in the connections between the regions and the EU Commission. The poorest regions of Europe can realize their interests least of all in the integration decisions, as the poor countries anyway have fewer representatives in the EU bodies. The competition policy of the EU also reinforces the effects of centralization, and community regional policy is less capable of counterbalancing the differences emanating from varying competitive abilities. Federal Germany is the best example of this; the regional regionalism and the decrease of spatial differences can also be matched at central government level.

In parallel with the irreversible deepening of European integration, the key positions of the national government are still retained, at least in three areas. One of the most important tasks of the state is to regulate capitalism in public companies, and industrial development, even in the future, cannot be imagined without effective national financial systems, as the safest starting point for corporate strategies will be the domestic market and the regulation environment also. The other important central government task remains the coordination of national innovation and technical development programs. Finally, as the third national level priority can be considered to be the labor market and industry-political tasks. Success in fulfilling these two latter national functions depends on how effective a part can subnational public administration play in fulfilling numerous partial tasks. Consequently, regionalization is, at the same time, a prerequisite for the successful operation of the nation-state, since macropolitical aims cannot be fulfilled without thoughtful human resources, educational training, and enterprise development; nor can well-balanced market competition be imagined without the cooperation of the social partners. The solution of these, however, is the most optimal at the level of the regions (Keating and Loughlin, 1997).

In Eastern and Central Europe today the future of the division of power between state and region still seems uncertain. The prospects for decentralization depend on the success of economic efficiency and the results of the "top to bottom" managed change of regime, but the preconditions at regional level for setting up power are unfavorable. In the former planned economies, the organizational framework deriving from strong centralization has remained, even if the substance of central power has changed a great deal. Even in the most favorable cases, the process of decentralization can be expected to be a long one.

Three possible ways of decentralization can be envisaged in Eastern and Central Europe, and each of these differs from the others in terms of the extent and quality of the division of power. The choice of way, naturally not an arbitrary one; the historical traditions of an individual country; the nature of the economic transformation; the establishment of institutions of the market economy; political power relations; and the degree of sophistication of the spatial structure all influence the decline of power concentration. The pressure to decentralize that falls on the central state administration is obviously stronger in those countries where the dynamic, regional major urban centers (for example, in Poland) wish to initiate their autonomous development, their structuring into the European regional division of labor, with the help of the (possibly, most liberalized) utilization of their internal resources and postindustrial development factors. However, the legitimization of bottom-up initiatives meets greater resistance in those countries (for example, in Hungary) where the central regions have a dominant, even a strengthening, position in the factors of production increasing competitiveness. Although the example of these two countries is a good one in demonstrating that the existence of regional centers capable of being made effective is no more than a potential advantage, the "suction effect" toward decentralization originating from the political legitimacy of Hungarian regional local authorities and the legal regulation of regional development can somehow counterbalance the lack of strong regional centers of appropriate European size.

In the first possible decentralization model, the division of labor between central and regional bodies is organized under clear, precise rules, and the development tasks for which the two types of body are responsible differ simply in respect of which regional unit these tasks affect. To solve these problems, regional authorities even have their own income resources and have wide-ranging rights in respect of planning, and the developments of local authorities that are part of their own circle can be subsidized from these (regional) funds. Depending on the economic development level of the region, "own" and "shared" income can be supplemented by transfers from central government funds. This strategy provides the most comprehensive form of decentralization, and, in the long term, this is the most effective solution. However, to create this, numerous—political, constitutional, public administrational, and economic—preconditions are necessary, and, even today, the progress of regional self-government in Eastern and Central Europe does not seem a realistic prospect. Further differentiation in the region will also derive from the fact that Poland and, hopefully, Hungary will take steps along the road to regionalism.

The gist of the second decentralization strategy model is that only certain functions (planning, development, executive, authorization, and financing) are transferred from the center to the regions, with the remaining regional, political tasks continuing within the competency of the central government. The expansion of the redistribution of power depends on the tasks that are to be decentralized, the institutional system that is to take them over, and the tools that will be at the disposal of the regions. This version is the best in the short term for those countries with a unitary system, since the preparations for transferring power need less effort, there being no need for a complete transformation of the public administration system, since the actual influence of the central bodies does not change (which is the most important consideration), and, as the management of regional development through deconcentrated state organization will be more complex, perhaps their efficiency will increase.

In the third option, the new division of responsibility between central and regional organs is based upon their handling of specific, occasional tasks. They create a common managing body for developing the peripheral, lagging regions, and the state provides part of its financial resources to this decision-making forum, whilst the execution of the development programs is delegated to the spatial units. This version represents the weakest version of decentralization, but, since there is no need to change the established power structure, it is not surprising that most Eastern and Central European countries have started to elaborate their spatial development programs on this basis. Central governments consider this solution as the easiest way to solve the problem: they do not need to put their hands into a hornet's nest and the vertical and horizontal power relations remain untouched.

## 3.5. Conclusions

The region is considered to be a spatial unit serving the sustainable growth of the economy and the modernization of the spatial structure, with independent financial resources, fulfilling autonomous development policy, and equipped with local government rights. On the basis of this term—whose factors naturally developed differently in the different periods of European development—regions have not so far existed in Eastern and Central Europe, despite the fact that some geographers (on the basis of the indisputable results obtained by geographic science in regional research) assert that we do possess some well-defined, natural regions. Such "form without content"— as in previous decades—cannot, in itself, steer the spatial structure of the country in a favorable direction, decentralize the new space-forming forces, and create the prerequisites for multipolar development. The region, if defined as a framework for regional research, is not capable of organizing the space-forming powers of the twenty-first century without the competencies, institutions, and tools.

Regions in the new member states are necessary, since European regional development clearly proves that a subnational level comprising approximately 1–2 million inhabitants regulated on the basis of self-government concepts (as a result of the region's economic capacity and structural abilities) is considered to b:

1. the optimal spatial framework for the realization of regional development policy, oriented toward economic development;
2. the appropriate field for the operation of postindustrial spatial organization forces, and the development of their interrelationships;
3. the important area in which to enforce regional and social interests;

4. the most appropriate size of spatial unit to build a modern infrastructure and the professional organizing-planning-executing institution of regional policy;
5. the main factor in the decision-making system of the European Union's Regional and Cohesion policy.

The decentralized state organization system can be created by organic development following complex legal regulation, but it would be desirable to have those concepts that generate the necessary preconditions laid down in the constitution (or, in case of a lack of consensus) in the Law on Decentralization)—namely:

1. the state, in its development activity and economic policy, builds on the interrelationships and conformities between the regional abilities and the spatial elements, and, by utilizing these, it provides the necessary conditions to exercise the basic social functions;
2. the state, in realizing the concept of social impartiality and justice, contributes with its own tools to a decrease in the objective, and, at the same time, large and constant, regional differences in creating equal opportunities for access to public services;
3. active regional policy on the part of the state promotes the regional decentralization of economic activities and functions;
4. the state shares its regional political tasks and tools with local authorities on the basis of precise rules, delegating regional coordination rights, and development resources to the regional authorities.

Naturally, creating political, public administration regions is a time-consuming task, but, in relation to the future, it was at this historically important time of the country's modernization prior to EU Accession that agreement should have been reached. At the same time, it has to be said that bitter political disputes do no favors to large-scale regional political reform, but, that apart, it is difficult to find arguments against the decentralizing trends of modernization and rationalization. Disputes notwithstanding, the target should be to submit to Parliament the basic documents necessary for changing to a regional public service and administration organization system—"the sooner the better."

The pressure for regionalization in Eastern and Central Europe today has been created not in relation to public administration or even for reason associated with EU membership. The increasing size of the economies, the modernization of the countries, the decline in regional differences, and the future of the positions to be gained in the Europe-wide regional division of labor constitute the stake. Regionalism can be the new motivating force for modernization at the beginning of the twenty-first century.

The current institutional system of regional development cannot even meet the original targets. Some regional agencies have the task of gathering projects together, and, consequently, they promote the carrying out of the will of central government and not the realization of regional concepts. In the performance of regional agencies, some basic differences can be seen. There are, for sure, some innovative examples willing to use the methods of modern regional economic development agencies, but there are also a number of traditional agencies operating in an executive role.

On the basis of empirical research, the greatest protest against the decentralized model has been provoked within the circle of the ministries. Balanced against this can be the fact that the majority of stakeholders involved in regional formation theoretically support reform, but are not convinced of the appropriateness of current regional borders and of regional centers, their regional relationships being in a narrower circle. It seems, however, in the opinion of the actors, that it is impossible to create regional borders more acceptable than the current ones, and it is most important not to distract attention from significant questions, such as the decentralization of the state and the strengthening of regional autonomy, with a debate about regional borders and the tug-of-war over regional centers. At the moment these last two questions are the ones that most excite the various county elite circles.

Never discussed or debated are the core questions such as: What functions should a region have? What responsibilities should central government pass to the regions? (Since the ministries also now realize that, perhaps, they are facing a change); Why does the central administration deal with the evaluation of an application for a couple of million forints? Whilst hundreds and thousands of applications are evaluated and ruled on, the same level of intensity is nowhere to be seen in any debate on strategic questions. Why is not the most important task for the central state administration to work out the sectoral operative programs so important for EU Accession? Why are there no intricately elaborated long-term development ideas?

Not only operative, but also important planning-strategy tasks can be delegated to the regions. This is rather more the case, since what is suggested by central offices will not be a realistic solution in the new programing period 2014–2020—namely, that the methods tested in one corner of the country can be used in another. Each region should be allowed to find its own way. Those EU member states are successful where the country is developing along different regional orbits.

To reduce underdevelopment and to develop the regions are the most important strategic aims of the European Community, and almost 40 percent of its budget is used for these purposes. For catching up, the member states, or, rather their regions (depending on their level of development), are given considerable support from the common budget. At the same time, we also have to see that, besides the large support in the ranking list of the regions in the individual member states, changes could only happen if, in the utilization of EU support, a long-term (several decades-long) structural policy were used. The regions in their development policy concentrated not on the development of traditional infrastructural elements, but on the modern regional development driving forces (innovation, business-services, modern industry-organization methods, and human resources development). Those regions that expected success exclusively from the EU's support policy and tried to fulfill the actual development policy aims at that specific moment, were unable to improve their relative position.

The basic concepts valid for all member states and related to fulfilling structural policy—subsidiarity, decentralization, in addition, concentration, programing, partnership, transparency—also demanded the modernization of the national-regional political institutional system, and these points of view must also be taken into account when the reform of public administration is being planned. The consistent application of these concepts in the EU member states has increased the efficiency of regional development and strengthened cohesion, and in the latest period a more frequently voiced new support policy aim, the development of competitiveness, is targeting the sustainable development of the regions. What is, perhaps, most important, is that the main aim of the EU's membership is not to obtain structural support, but to exploit the privileges of the 450 million market. Deriving from this is that the method for further development of regional policy should be found not merely (and exclusively) in the expansion of redistribution, but in the opportunities for mobilizing resources.

In most EU member states today, it is obvious that the division of power and the institutions of multilevel government increase both the economic performance capacity and welfare in the individual regions. The lobbyist politician will be replaced by the developer-type politician who regulates, with directives and laws, the long-term guarantees of local autonomous development, who promotes European cooperation, and builds partnership connections among the region's actors. The success of this approach is proved by the successful development of numerous West European regions and by its outstanding role as the creator of regional identity.

## REFERENCES

A. Amin, A., and J. Tomaney (1995) "The regional dilemma in a neo-liberal Europe," in *European Urban and Regional Studies*, 2, 171–88.

Bachtler, J., R. Downes, and G. Gorzelak (eds.) (2000) *Transition, Cohesion and Regional Policy in Central and Eastern Europe* (Aldershot: Ashgate).

Blažek, J., and S. Boeckhout (2000) "Regional policy in the Czech Republic and EU accession" in J. Bachtler, R. Downes, and G. Gorzelak (eds.), *Transition, Cohesion and Regional Policy in Central and Eastern Europe* (London: Ashgate), 301–18.

Dostál, P. (2000) "Reintegrating Central European region: Challenges of trans-border spatial development" in *Acta Universitatis Carolinae. Geographica*, 1, 21–38.

Geshev, G. (2001) "The role of regions of South-Eastern space in the enlarging European Union," in Z. Gál (ed.), *Role of the Regions in the Enlarging European Union* (Pécs: Centre for Regional Studies, Discussion Papers, Special Issue).

Horváth, Gy. (ed.) (2003) *Székelyföld* (Budapest and Pécs,: MTA Regionális Kutatások Központja).

Horváth, Gy. (1996) "Transition and regionalism in East-Central Europe. Tübingen, Europäischen Zentrum für Föderalismus-Forschung" in *Occasional Papers*, 7.

Illner, M. (2000) "Issues of decentralization. Reforms in former communist countries" in *Infomationen zur Raumforschung*, 7–8, 391–401.

Keating, M., and Loughlin J. M. (eds.) (1997) *The Political Economy of Regionalism* (London: Frank Cass).

Kovács, Pálné I. (2007) "Disintegrated (or fragmented) public administration and regional policy in Eastern Europe" in P. Getimis and G. Kafkalas, (eds.), *Overcoming Fragmentation in Southeast Europe. Spatial Development Trends and Integration Potential* (Aldershot: Ashgate), 75–100.

Späth, L. (1989) *1992—Der Traum von Europa* (Stuttgart: Deutsche Verlags-Anstalt).

Späth, L. (1991) *1992—Európa álma* (Budapest: Közgazdasági és Jogi Könyvkiadó).

Szreniawski, P. (2004) "Regions in Poland" in Gy. Enyedi and I. Tózsa (eds.), *Region. Regional Development Policy, Administration and E-government* (Budapest: Akadémiai Kiadó), 277–92.

Tariska, M. (2004) "Regional administration in the Slovak Republic" in Gy. Enyedi and I. Tózsa (eds.), *Region. Regional Development Policy, Administration and E-government* (Budapest: Akadémiai Kiadó), 310–41.

# 4

# AN UNFINISHED JOURNEY—LOMBARDY ON THE ROAD TO DECENTRALIZATION[1]

## Balázs Lóránd

### 4.1. INTRODUCTION

The aim of the study is to analyze the *Lombard model of governance* and to highlight the most important factors behind its success. To investigate the situation in which it was possible to introduce the principle of subsidiarity, we look at the enhanced possibilities for the Italian regions. Although autonomy is not as significant as was demanded by the region, it is sufficient to develop an "own governance" model at least on an experimental basis.

The model is a success in the region, although there are internal and external *risks* that have to be countered. The failures of the "quasi market," the need for further evaluation, the operation of networks in civil society, cooperation among public actors, the limited visibility of the region, and the mentality of public administration are all significant internal elements of the model. From outside, fiscal uncertainty, unbalanced federalism, the development gap between Lombardy and the rest of Italy, and new challenges all have an impact on the operation of the Lombard model of governance, and to support efforts to cope with these challenges we highlight possible solutions—in general, but especially in the field of state-society relationships and quasi-market features.

The interesting issue is whether this model could be *implemented* in any other areas of Europe, and, to deal with this, the focus should be on the systematic approach, which means that the social and economic background, the driving principle, and willingness, are sufficient only in total to foster the development of the Lombard model. In general, the model is strictly territory-based and path dependency is crucial in such a situation.

## 4.2. Growing Possibilities for Regions in Italy

In recent decades the process of decentralization in Italy has proved to be both highly complex and confused, and it is *still unfinished*: the constitutional reform of 2001 has not yet been implemented thoroughly. It is an interesting situation that the huge differences in development within the country and the serious redistribution process among the regions are, at the same time, both cause and obstacle in the decentralization process (Ambrosanio et al., 2010).

In Italy it is very challenging for the regions to find their *own place and identity* in the political area between the communes, the provinces, and the state (the national government) (Horváth, 1993). Furthermore, there is a strong tradition of centralization, which is embedded precisely in political practice and state bureaucracy (Keating, 1997). Thanks to the reforms, the autonomy of the regions has strengthened and today there is more authority to differentiate their policies and to shape regional administration, own identity and space, political leadership, visibility, and legitimacy (Colombo, 2008).

From the 1990s more and more power was devolved to the level of regions, together with the necessary financial instruments, although, at a certain point, the process stopped. Now the regions are fighting for more competencies, since they cannot implement programs or intervene in regulations without the right to do so and without the necessary financial resources.

In the twenty-first century there is a general tendency that is having an effect on regionalism: the *changing role of the state*. The dismantling of traditional borders and instruments (increased mobility, unlimited and uncontrolled flow of information, etc.) foster the creation of a new framework, which is more favorable in relation to current conditions. *Regionalization* could be an appropriate answer in this situation (Interv. *Bassetti*).

After analyzing these issues of regionalism, the question arises of how effective the autonomy of the Italian regions has been. The answer depends heavily on the *ambitions, ideals, and capabilities* of the individual regions, and so the distinctive ideology of a regional government is crucial (Colombo, 2008). In general terms, the Italian "limited system of constitutional regionalism" (Hopkins, 2002, p. 110.) offers the opportunity for the regions to find their own governmental solutions, internal system configurations, strategic directions for the future, and their own identity and ideas to guide them on their way forward along the path of decentralization and federalism.

## 4.3. THE LOMBARD MODEL

### 4.3.1. Subsidiarity as a Driving Principle

Due to the opportunities for regions to establish their own government system and philosophy, Lombardy has made the best of these opportunities by using the principle of subsidiarity. This principle has a great importance in the Lombard model, because it is the main *driving principle*, it is the central idea, which is cited and used in a lot of sectors with, of course, different results and success.

Applying this principle to a governance model offers a real *alternative* to the existing state-market combinations. The basic concept is trust between parties. The effect of the model is to enhance responsibility on both sides, and it may revitalize the actors of both state and market. The state's results-oriented behavior is obligatory and the dynamics of market forces are extended to previously untouched sectors (Brugnoli and Vittadini, 2009).

Whilst the principle is implemented the government should not answer or fulfill every need, but ought to *create the necessary conditions* for civil society to fulfill them. In this respect, the freedom of initiative and the responsibility of the single person or organization are fundamental. This attitude can bring value for the whole of society (Interv. *Intiglietta*). Subsidiarity is not only a suitable method to deliver growth and prosperity but also essential to support and deliver the needs of the local community. In this manner, the essence is not only economic growth but welfare and the quality of life as well (Kitson, 2009).

Using the principle of subsidiarity, a very important factor is to improve processes and services, and so to find the *best level* to fulfill a need, where the issues can be better handled. This can sometimes mean raising the required competence levels rather than lowering them (Interv. *Violini*).

### 4.3.2. The Region and the Strength of its Background

Lombardy as a region has very *strong economic, social structures* and so is one of the most developed areas of Europe, the wealthiest region of Italy. These features have built up a critical background for the implementation of the subsidiarity principle.

Lombardy has been one of the wealthiest regions in Europe for hundreds of years and has always played an *important role* in the Italian economic system, both as a market for goods and as a producer of a wide range of quality products. Similarly it has been Italy's window on Europe, a central point of the exchange of ideas, people, and goods between Italy and the rest of Europe (Mussati, 1993). In the Lombard region we find the highest concentration of people, businesses, and wealth in Italy. This amounts to precisely 15.6 percent of the total population of the country (9.5 million inhabitants), 20 percent of Italy's gross domestic product (GDP) (€32,128 per capita), and 15 percent of all national enterprises are located here (809,000). Further, Lombardy is the major financial center of Italy, and a huge number of voluntary associations and nonprofit organizations are based in the region (Colombo, 2008; IReR, 2009a).

According to the opinions of the region's stakeholders, the strength of the Lombard economy is rooted in *culture and tradition*: Catholic, socialist, and liberal ideals. Lombard people are naturally ready to take risks. In the nineteenth and twentieth centuries this approach also created the means to support this kind of activity. In general, Lombards are characterized by their natural aptitude for entrepreneurship (Interv. *Intiglietta*).

*Innovation and knowledge transfer* are two of the flagships of the region (Interv. *Rappelli*). In Lombardy the best sector of the Italian scientific system is located, with top universities and leading research centers. A significant part of the Lombard economy is based on science-based industries, and the very positive attitude toward cooperation is a perfect base for collective learning processes and innovation (Mussati, 1993). The knowledge base of the region and the economy is extraordinarily strong: here are the highest number of universities (12), and 21 percent of Italy's expenditure on R&D is spent here (IReR, 2009a).

An ageing population, a high rate of immigration, the obsolescence of the existing system of professional training, environmental problems (urban sprawl, traffic congestion, pollution), postindustrialization of the economy (skill bottlenecks) are significant *challenges* for Lombardy (Colombo, 2008). From an economic point of view, it is essential for the region, for its future prosperity, to improve its knowledge-based economy; it must exploit skills, ideas, and networks. To achieve this, Lombardy needs a high degree of local interactions (Kitson, 2009).

### 4.3.3. The Role of Regional Government in Lombardy

The Lombard region (as other normal regions) *shares competence and lawmaking powers* with the national Parliament and government in many fields: e.g., in foreign trade, the labour market, education, health, research, major transport infrastructure, energy, communications, the environment, and culture. In these areas the region has administrative-regulative competence, whilst the state determines only general policy principles. There are, also, areas of absolute state competence—in, for example, foreign affairs, defense, currency, savings, social security, and the national heritage. In other fields the regions have opportunities to acquire increased or exclusive competence. Further, the state cannot override regional legislation (IReR, 2009a).

The head of the regional government bears the title of president and since 1999 has been elected directly by the population. He is the leader of the executive, responsible for the policies adopted by the council and he appoints the ministers. The regional council is the assembly that directly represents the citizens, defines regional policy, and enacts legislation. It has eighty members. The administration supports the work of the president and ministers and consists of Directorates General (departments), which are responsible for management and operational issues, whilst, for efficient vertical coordination, there are numerous committees handling cross-sectional affairs. The entire system fosters flexibility, well-elaborated planning, and the integration of responsibility for financial resources and personnel (IReR, 2009a).

The efficiency of the government, which is generally respected, is measurable by its *per capita expenditure* and the relative size of the administration. The administrative staff of the Lombard region is much smaller in numbers than, for example, that of Campania.[2] Only 3.9 percent of GDP is spent by the regional government in Lombardy and this inadequate budget means that the region must find innovative ways to meet its needs. The annual cost of administration is €80 per citizen (IReR, 2009b).

In recent years, serious *cuts* were made in Lombard's bureaucracy. First, the number of regional government employees was reduced from 4,500 to 3,000 and the number of executives was reduced from 600 to 250. This meant 31 officials per 100,000 population, little more than one-third of the average of the Italian regions (83). Second, 1995 saw the introduction of legislative consolidation. The Consolidation Acts slashed the number of laws then in force from 2,000 to a 2009 figure of 300. With more or less universal computerization, the length of time taken for administrative procedures, important for both citizens and companies, has also drastically reduced (IReR, 2009b).

A recent study calculated the regional distribution of *public expenditure* for the year 2005. This showed total expenditure in Lombardy (per capita) of €9,444, whilst the average for Italy was €9,488. A breakdown of these figures shows that, for health and education, expenditure is relatively consistent at regional level, although it varies for social security and other functions (material purchases, economic affairs, environmental protection, housing and community amenities, recreation, culture, and religion). In Lombardy, spending on health and education (€2,229) is below the national average (€2,400), whilst on social security (€4,819) it is above average (€4,432). At the same time, for other sectors the region's figure of €1,236 is well below the national average of €1,496, and the third lowest of all—only the Veneto and Puglia being lower (Ambrosanio et al., 2010).

In respect of the characteristics of regional government, it is important to highlight the fact that, in Lombardy, there is constant pressure on the bureaucracy to be *innovative* and to adapt to the changing needs of the population. Evaluating activity is of key importance and it is increasingly common to have ideas for evaluation and to evaluate them. To improve these features still further, the government is trying to promote the appropriate culture, and Éupolis Lombardia provides training for administration personnel (relating to indicators and the significance of different results and impacts). The mentality and culture of the regional authority's public sector is an excellent example for other regions. Further, Lombardy is willing to import new ideas, in attempts to improve actual practice. Lombardy must still face the basic challenge of maintaining accountability and openness, but a main factor is knowledge: public sector managers should be fully aware of the situation over their territory (Interv. *Sbrissa*).

### 4.3.4. Implementation of the Subsidiarity Principle in Lombardy

In many ways Lombardy is a *pioneer region*. The reform process concentrates on issues of devolution, horizontal subsidiarity, and the empowerment of citizens, and the levels affected by changes are public policy and the operation of government organizations (Armajani, 2009).

An unusual degree of stability can be seen in the political history of the region, where Formigoni has been president since 1995 (IReR, 2009b), and the Forza Italia (now People of Freedom) party dominates the coalition in the regional assembly. Formigoni brought the distinctive but unifying idea of subsidiarity to the region, and this acts as a key to many major reforms. The governance is influenced by the principle of subsidiarity to an unusual degree (Colombo, 2008).[3]

In fact the notion and practice of subsidiarity have been implemented seriously and innovatively for the last fifteen years and with the clear main principles of *freedom and responsibility* (IReR, 2009b). The aim of the government is to recognize needs and to try to help meet them by organizing initiatives. Responding to the needs is crucial, but satisfying them completely is not the aim—which, in fact, is to enhance the value of the answers that the community has already given to the needs of people. It is, therefore, not the regional government that fulfills the needs of the people; rather, it organizes and brings together all the resources and solutions coming from the public and private sectors and from NGOs (Interv. *Intiglietta*). During the implementation of the subsidiarity principle a learning process is evident—one that displays constant, creative adaptation and permanent logic. This development is not automatic, and so the role of evaluation is essential (Brugnoli and Vittadini, 2009).

This concept has been implemented in many sectors—naturally, with varying results. The effort to build up an ideological background to policies was probably more *successful* in Lombardy than in other regions (Interv. *Dente*). This solution could be useful in a situation where financial resources are limited and where the needs of the population are growing. Under these circumstances state action is not enough. In order to maintain universality as a main characteristic of European welfare, subsidiarity is the best way owing to its closeness to the level where the services are needed, which improves the efficiency, the effectiveness, and the fairness of their management (Interv. *Vittadini*).[4]

In the Lombard model, horizontal subsidiarity means the *involvement* of small and intermediate units of society such as the family, church, and voluntary associations. This is a form of bottom-up decentralization. The relationship between the state and the actors is contractual (Powell, 2007). Notable aspects of the Lombard model are relationships, which are "at the heart of what makes for a good life" (Leadbeater, 2009, p. 80). In any society the skills of listening, understanding, and working together are as remarkable as reading and writing. The solution in Lombardy is to build up a model of the relationship-based state, and strengthening participation and relationships produces a more legitimate state. To have a workable situation in the partnerships driven by the subsidiarity principle, knowledge, action, and control are the critical elements, although usually control is neglected (Interv. *Ceriani*).

The future of subsidiarity is that it becomes a *system*, a form of institutionalized government. The rules in the political and public

fields should be redefined. After the first steps, the system seems sufficiently mature and established, and so further institutionalization
of the experience is possible (Brugnoli and Vittadini, 2009), and
after the successful implementation of the model in Lombardy, the
model is exportable to other parts of Europe, although only under
certain circumstances, which we will examine later in the study.

### 4.3.5. Solutions for the Implementation of Subsidiarity: The Relations to the Quasi Market

In the Lombard model of governance, subsidiarity forms the ideological background and the quasi market is the implementation level—
although these two expressions do not mean the same thing. In a
quasi-market structure profit must exist, but in a subsidiarity model
there could be nonprofit solutions and providers also. In a quasi market the keywords are accreditation and evaluation, competition and
freedom of choice and financial relationship. In a subsidiarity model
there are additional important features: freedom, opportunity, trust,
and responsibility (see Figure 4.1).

The quasi-market structure is more *rigid;* the subsidiarity principle
provides more room for *experimenting.* Further, recognition is more
necessary in subsidiarity: that is, the public sector should acknowl-
edge the existing solutions of the private sector and support them
by covering their costs (this creates a partnership). In a simple quasi-
market structure the public authorities set the rules and guidelines.
Therefore, the definition of needs is radically different for the two
solutions: in a quasi market the state decides what is important for
the citizens and calls for help from private actors, since they are more
efficient and less expensive. In a subsidiarity model, the state asks
society what it needs and creates a partnership with private providers
to fulfill the desires (Interv. *Ceriani*).

The *voucher system* means that the government gives support direct
to the user (in case of schools to the families of the pupils), and so
everyone is entitled to an amount of money, and it is the individual
who decides in which school he will undergo the training program.
Therefore, schools managed by private companies or associations are
also entitled to public funds, since they have pupils with vouchers
(Interv. *Intiglietta*). This mechanism also applies to social care.

An interesting point in relation to this topic is that, to implement
subsidiarity and to have a quasi market, a *real market* (with a critical
mass of users) is necessary with demand. In small towns or in the
provinces the market is relatively small—which means that the private

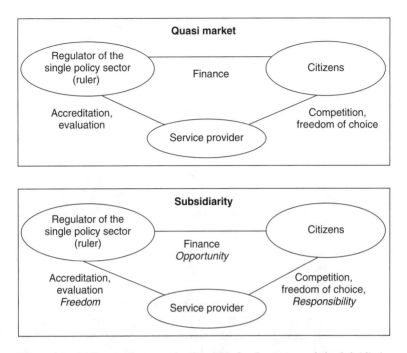

**Figure 4.1**  Differences between the Quasi-Market Structure and the Subsidiarity Model

*Source*: Author's elaboration of Barattieri (unpublished), 2011.

providers of local-scale services may not always be interested in fulfilling every need of this market. Consequently, the public sector should handle the situation. This is a serious limitation, although it does not undermine the validity of the model.

### 4.3.6. The Lombard Model of Governance

After analyzing the features of the model, we framed the *exact model* from our perspective (see Figure 4.2). To our mind, the model is based on three basic elements: the social and economic background, the innovative way of governance, and the principle of subsidiarity. The importance of a strong civil society and highly developed economic structures foster the evolution of an appropriate mentality among the population (both individuals and communities) and sustain the necessary (human and financial) resources for the policies. The innovativeness of governance and openness toward the new provisions are requisite for the Lombard model. Subsidiarity connects

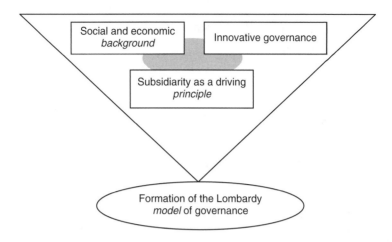

**Figure 4.2**    The Lombard Model of Governance
*Source:* Designed by Balázs Lóránd, 2011.

all of these elements into a well-prepared, high-level system and high-lights the way to implement the model as a driving principle. It is the mixture of all these features that creates the appropriate conditions for the formulation of the model. It produces a model of governance in the sense of an organizational system, as practical solutions in different policy areas and as a general driving philosophy.

## 4.4. Risks Inherent in the Model

### 4.4.1. From Inside the System

There are many (previously mentioned) advantages of the Lombard model relating to civil society, to the welfare sector, and so on. We propose, however, to present the areas that we see as *problematic*, and which, therefore, mean risk, due to the basic nature of the current system. It is possible to distinguish between the risks: there are elements connected to the socioeconomic context of Lombardy (the first four), and there are others that have a relation to policy and institutional issues (the final three).

#### 4.4.1.1. Lack of Policy Evaluation in the System
*Transparent and effective auditing* is vital (Interv. *Ceriani*), since, in many cases, public money is used in civil society. In this area much still remains to be done and "independent mechanisms of control

and evaluation" (Colombo and Mazzoleni, 2007, p. 81) are necessary. Currently it is the regional government that decides, implements, and evaluates policy (and the accompanying risks) by selecting audit methods (A further interesting question would be whether an *index of subsidiarity* should be set up for Lombardy to evaluate its policies in relation to subsidiarity).

Generally, an *independent system of performance evaluation* is relevant in every welfare sector and when public policies are involved. In the health-care system, a reasonably suitable quality assessment system does exist, but it is based only on procedures and not on effectiveness. The basic question is whether an evaluation of effectiveness is workable in this context (Interv. *Violini*).

### 4.4.1.2. *"Cream-Skimming" and the "Quasi" Quasi Market*

Real competition is vital if we are to have a quasi market, and for this the openness of the market is crucial: to ensure that *new providers* can enter the market easily. "Cream-skimming" is common practice. In a situation where a private provider (school, hospital, or other entity) can select its users and serve the least expensive, this could produce such a situation. One solution would be to be aware of the problem and knowledgeable enough to prevent it happening (Interv. *Ceriani*). To do this, further regulation (and subsidy) would be needed for those supplying the more expensive users, and so "opportunities and incentives for selection or cream-skimming must be eliminated" (Le Grand, 2007, p. 77).

A "quasi" quasi market exists in Italy (Interv. *Rappelli*). The system was established successfully in Lombardy, but there are a number of significant problems such as the *path dependency of traditional policies, corporate resistance, and bureaucratic practice*. For example, public hospitals are not allowed to close even if they have no patients, since they are financed by the state, irrespective of the volume of services provided (Colombo, 2008).

### 4.4.1.3. *Centralization inside the Networks*

*Ever-changing and increasing human needs and desires* foster the appearance of new social entrepreneurs, and each social firm or organization has its own specific attitude. For example, some years ago a most serious problem was drug dependency, and so there was a blossoming of social entrepreneurship in this field. Today this problem is not so serious and so many of these firms have lost their raison d'être. As a result, the social market is unstable, each successive period having its own challenge. This involves what we may term "social correction" for the oligarchic risk (Interv. *Rovati*). Societies that are sufficiently strong and rich in initiative (such as Lombardy) are strong enough to resist oligarchic trends.

Nevertheless, inside the third sector there are some important networks of small or large associations[5] that are able to apply for more significant programs and which also have a greater chance of succeeding in winning them. This results in a kind of partnership among the actors. These networks are enormously important bodies, able to negotiate directly with regional institutions or with regional government. The problematic issue is the representative nature of the smaller organizations—something that could lead to centralization within the major networks. The principle of subsidiarity requires an open market, but fewer advantages are left for the latecomers than for those first on the scene. This is a clear risk that institutions have to bear in mind. There are, of course, different solutions to the operation of networks. For example, if they are organized with an open mind and with a strong inclination toward social creativity, then there is an open space for participation. If, however, it is managed in an authoritarian and centralized way, then it will reduce the democracy of the system (Interv. *Rovati*).

### 4.4.1.4. Not Enough Cooperation among Actors and Institutions in the Public Sector

Within the public sector, the level of cooperation among the different institutions is too low. The Chamber of Commerce has attempted to develop a role for itself in this field, but has been only partially successful. The explanation for this is that the institutions think that they do not need to cooperate: it is usually policy-dependent (Interv. *Dente*). The problem is also visible between different levels of government when state and region have a shared competence.

### 4.4.1.5. Limited Visibility of the Region among Citizens

A general problem of democracies today is that people are not sufficiently interested in what is happening at government level (*"crises of democracy"*). The information is too much for them. The task of public institutions is to highlight the most important information, to show the situation to citizens (complete with evaluation), and to monitor the results.

The visibility of the regional level is related to this: municipalities and provinces have existed for two hundred years in Italy, but regions were only created in the 1970s. Among people, in general, there is simply not enough information about the real tasks of the intermediate level between local and central government. There are virtually no media working with the regions, which means a lack of any regional public arena. Citizens know the name of the president of the region (Interv. *Rappelli*) and that health is the responsibility of the region. This could lead to accountability problems, although it is, of course, a mainly Italian phenomenon.

Lombardy does not recognize itself clearly enough as a region. In Italy, local identity is, in general, quite strong, but there is no firm identification with an administrative region such as Lombardy, even among the voters of the League (Keating, 1997). Further, given the region's outstanding role in the national economy, it is doubtful whether a regional-level interest in Lombardy could be used as a negotiating base (Colombo and Mazzoleni, 2007).

### 4.4.1.6. Not Automatic Mechanism: A Step-by-Step Process

To have a complete model of subsidiarity in operation in Lombardy is no easy task, and there are many other areas for *further development*. Subsidiarity can work in the region, although numerous further steps are needed to achieve the goal. Besides, there are no automatic mechanisms to foster the implementation of the model, which is a true step-by-step process. Subsidiarity can work, but there is a need for evaluation and control (Interv. *Ceriani*).

### 4.4.1.7. Mentality of Public Administration

The structure of national and local bureaucracy in Italy is traditionally *hostile to innovation* (evolved from the Napoleonic imprint). Among these are mainly high-ranking, civil servants with a legal educational background and there are many regulations covering all aspects of life. The reform system nowadays is *rigid and slow*—not adaptable to the managerial perspective (to stress results over procedures) (Colombo, 2008).

With regulations, the way in which the administration works can be altered, but it takes generations to change the mentality of the people (Interv. *Rappelli*). Accountability and evaluation are also important in this field. Sometimes people refuse to be evaluated, because of the mentality originated from bureaucracy (Interv. *Vittadini*).

## 4.4.2. From Outside

### 4.4.2.1. Fiscal Uncertainty (Timing, Complexity, Amount of Redistribution)

There are three main problems concerning the finance of the regions. First of all, there is *timing*, which means that taxes are collected by the state and taken from regional to national level, where the government decides how much money should be assigned to health-care and other services. The process is quite difficult to track and the national level can never be relied upon to deliver the funds to the regions on time. This results in uncertainty (Interv. *Sbrissa*).

Second, the effective and efficient operation of the region is not supported by the actual instruments of tax-collecting and redistribution. From a technical aspect, more innovative instruments are needed to simplify regional financing procedures (Interv. *Sbrissa*).

Third, there is a high *redistribution* factor from Lombardy, which means that only 22–23 percent of the taxes produced in the region are returned from the central budget.[6] Solidarity is an important factor, but further development demands a more realistic balance, since, otherwise, the competitiveness of Lombardy will be damaged and it will not be able to support the less developed regions of the country. There is, in fact, in Lombardy, a huge need to improve the infrastructure, to develop roads and railways (Interv. *Sbrissa*). There is also a continuous dispute between the regions and the state about adequate finance for regional competences.

### 4.4.2.2. Two-Faced Federalism

To implement federalism, regional resources are necessary. Responsibility in this field means that, if you handle your own resources, you are more efficient (Interv. *Bassetti*). Currently, *fiscal autonomy* in Italy is, in many ways, ambivalent. Most of the regions' revenue still comes from the state based on uniform criteria—regulated and determined by national legislation, and collected by the state. A region retains the whole of the regional business tax and vehicle tax collected. It also has the right to levy a supplementary tax on petrol and charge an additional tax to support health service. This, of course, means regional autonomy, although, in Italy, there is a system of national tax equalization (IReR, 2009a). There is a need in Lombardy for full fiscal subsidiarity, since this determines the degree of autonomy (Colombo, 2008).

In fact, decisions on *expenditure* (and investments and financial control) are still *centralized* and 68.2 percent of expenditure is devoted to health care. Regional government controls only 10 percent of total public expenditure in the region, the remainder being for state and municipal purposes. Regional structures and services take 3.9 percent of the GDP of Lombardy, and staff (approximately 5,000 people) represents no more than 12 percent of all state employees in the region.

As for cost and budgetary control, although the health system's deficit has been significantly reduced, the financial pressures are large. Welfare measures mean immediate costs for the budget of the regional government, and these cannot be covered by increased revenues due to the absence of fee-charging and tax-raising autonomy. Further, the effects of competition are blunted by bureaucratic resistance and employment protection legislation in the public sector (Colombo, 2008).

One of the most important problems is that regional autonomy has increased, but *political federalism* has not come about. Further, most regional income comes from transfers from the center. There are local taxes and duties in the system, but national tax equalization distorts the allocation (Powell, 2007). The willingness to have a decentralized country is very much in the focus of the wealthier regions, but these are not politically dominant in the country, and especially in Italy—Lombardy (Keating, 1997).

### 4.4.2.3. The Development Gap between Lombardy and the Rest of Italy

Lombardy has been a *donor* to Italy for many years and it must provide resources to other regions, since it is the richest in Italy (Interv. *Ceriani*). The problem of redistribution is mainly that, in many regions, the public administration generally utilizes public resources *inefficiently*. This heads to a scarcity of resources allocated to the poorest areas. Solidarity is a necessary issue, but the need for efficiency should be of the highest importance in those regions (Interv. *Vittadini*).

The relatively high differences within Italy result in fiscal flows among the regions (Ambrosanio et al., 2010, p. 98). Concerning the findings of a recent study[7] in Italy, which is largely consistent with other existing findings, sound financial flows are visible from the rich northern to the poor southern regions. This means that a citizen of Lombardy pays 30 percent of his or her taxes to support other regions. The study also proved that the total expenditure is higher in the north and tax revenue is lower in the south (Ambrosanio et al., 2010).

The public sector generally works to equalize current per capita public expenditure, at least in relation to basic services, although the process is not yet complete. Thanks to the great gaps in economic development levels of the regions, and the huge differences in the amount of tax revenues, partial equalization generates regular fiscal flows. According to an up-to-date study, convergence among regions in Italy (which stopped in the 1970s) is needed to provide some hope of fiscal federalism. The question is whether these fiscal flows are sustainable in the financial crisis and despite the investment needs of the north (Ambrosanio et al., 2010).

The solution could be to organize more *national framework programs* within Italy, instead of supporting the southern regions with more funds—which means a greater help for the less developed areas (Interv. *Rappelli*).

#### 4.4.2.4. No Inner Benchmark Possibilities

The model of Lombardy has potentially wide implications. The evaluation of the goals and comparison with other examples is necessary for further learning (Powell, 2007). Although it is a serious problem that the Lombard model is unique in Italy, the solutions applied here are far ahead of what has been done in other regions. There is a real risk: no comparison is available (Interv. *Sbrissa*), and so improvements to the system must be totally innovative.

#### 4.4.2.5. New Challenges

As the Lombard model evolves, there are new challenges from *society and the economy* that have an impact on the region. Unemployment is rising, but mainly due to the economic crisis. Gender issues are a serious problem: how could women handle the double burden of job and family. A central issue is that of the "Mama-hotel," which means that young people stay in the parental home until the age of thirty-five/thirty-six. They have only temporary work (most new jobs are temporary), do not invest in their future, and will not marry. Their salary is lower and their future is unpredictable (Interv. *Rappelli*). Young people need to adjust to this period and learn how to handle it.

A further important challenge is that the territory is not as significant as it is used to be. In the age of *"glocalization"* (expressing globalization and localization at the same time), the world cannot be reorganized starting from the territory. This means a global crisis for the traditional states where borders have disappeared, sovereignty does not exist, the time and cost of mobility is heavily reduced, and an unlimited flow of information is common. There is a need for a response (Interv. *Bassetti*), and perhaps regionalism and the convergence of multilevel governance could be a solution.

## 4.5. FACING THE CHALLENGES

### 4.5.1. State-Society Relations

Some of the risks highlight the importance of *state-society relations*. Generally, governments and states have serious and powerful roles in contemporary society (Leicht and Jenkins, 2010), although there are important elements in this relationship to be analyzed further and to emphasize the main solution for the Lombard model of governance.

The *autonomy* of the state is significantly influenced by the society in which it is embedded. Social control of the state is essential, since greater control produces more currency (compliance, participation, legitimacy) for the leaders of the state (Migdal, 2004). There is a strong interdependence between state and society: society provides important elements for the state to be effective and the state is crucial in fostering collective action in society (Sellers, 2010).

Besides making and enforcing regulations, there is an opportunity for the state to delegate authority to other mechanisms, that is, the church or the market (Migdal, 2004). New *configurations* are being formulated between state and society, which mean the mobilization of special groups, the engagement of the third sector to deliver social services, and decentralization to open new local channels for coopera-tion between state and society. Enhanced accountability and partici-pation could be an alternative to marketization (Sellers, 2010).

All in all, to face the challenges, the solution could be to build up and further strengthen the network of civil activists and government leaders, to foster the participation of more and more citizens, to apply various solutions to each policy sector depending on its nature, and to communicate thoroughly and systematically the values of society.

### 4.5.2. Coping with the Problems of the Quasi Market

For a successful quasi market, different *conditions* are required. First, real competition is needed, which means several accessible providers without a monopoly or oligopoly structure (Brugnoli and Vittadini, 2009). Customer sovereignty could be compromised if there were only a few competitors (Lowery, 1998). Further, there should also be many potential buyers (Le Grand, 2007). Second, programming and providing should be separated institutionally, with providing being in the hands of the private sector. Third, users and suppliers need to be well informed about the possibilities of the system (Brugnoli and Vittadini, 2009). Providers and purchasers must also have access to accurate and independent information about the services (Powell, 2003). Fourth, transactional costs should be low and the users need to have access to services without restriction. Fifth, cream-skimming should be avoided by compensating the providers dealing with more expensive users. Sixth, a strict evaluation system is necessary deal-ing with the quality and quantity of the services provided (Brugnoli and Vittadini, 2009). Last, the motivation of the providers should be reconsidered. Nonprofit providers' motivation is not strictly connected to financial terms, and so could be unclear. Sometimes there are third parties acting on behalf of the users, whose interests could differ from the users' (Powell, 2003). "What is needed is well-designed public policies, ones that employ market-type mechanisms but which do not allow unfettered self-interest to dominate altruistic motivations" (Le Grand, 2003, p. 168).

Therefore, in Lombardy, to face the challenges of the quasi market, there is a need to foster (financially) the third sector and for private actors to establish provider organizations in unattached sectors and territories—which could generate a real competition. Further, the strengthening of the information flow toward users about the services and providers is essential. Regulations against cream-skimming should be fostered further and some innovative, experimental solutions should be initiated for the longer term.

## 4.6. GENERAL SUGGESTIONS

To handle these risks and to strengthen the system of governance, the following steps could be useful in Lombardy:

1. Applying revolutionary solutions in the different policy fields and trying to use *experimentation* as a regular method for the further development of the mechanisms and interventions of the region.
2. Collecting and utilizing more *benchmarks* from the UK, the Nordic countries, and the United States.
3. *Popularizing* the Lombard model of governance amongst Italians nationwide and trying to make citizens conscious of the role of civil society and the state in the twenty-first century.
4. Fostering openness among the policy actors (politicians and managers) by sending them abroad to participate in *postgraduate programs* of public policy to learn more about "best practice."
5. Disseminating the *best solutions* observed in specific areas by fostering the civil sector's initiatives in new fields.

### 4.6.1. Implementation Issues for Central and Eastern Europe

The Lombard model of governance is also *territory-based*. "What works in one place, might not work in another" (Brugnoli and Vittadini, 2009, p. 66). Other regions adopted certain Lombard initiatives, but no *systematic influence has yet been realized*. The Lombard model builds on the existence of distinct regional social capital. In general, it "has wrestled the 3 main principles of social regulation": the authority of the state, the operation of the market, and community solidarity (Colombo, 2008).

The implementation of the model in other countries heavily depends on a *very active private sector:* in which a mixture of for-profit and nonprofit organizations is essential. The serious dilemma is how the division of labor should be between the public and private sectors. Regional and national policy could do much in this field, but without the strength of civil society and private initiative, it would not be enough. The ability to create things has played a fundamental role in Lombardy (Interv. *Dente*).

As regards exporting the model to Central and Eastern Europe, a *systematic approach* is important. There is a need to develop the civil sector, and to foster the establishment of a civil society encouraged by progress. Opportunity, responsibility, and freedom are, once again, the keywords.

## NOTES

1. I would like to thank all the people I interviewed in Milan in June 2010: Giancarlo Rovati, professor, Università Cattolica del Sacro Cuore; Alberto Ceriani, senior researcher, Istituto Regionale di Ricerca della Lombardia; Federico Rappelli, consultant, Istituto Regionale di Ricerca della Lombardia; Bruno Dente, professor, Politecnico di Milano and Istituto per la ricerca sociale; Piero Bassetti, president, Globus et Locus; Neva Sbrissa, director, Coordination Unit, Lombardy Regional Government; Lorenza Violini, professor, Università degli Studi di Milano; Antonio Intiglietta, coordinator, Compagnia delle Opere Lombardy; Giorgio Vittadini, professor, Università degli Studi Milano Bicocca and Fondazione per la Sussidiarietà.

2. Previously people were hired in the public sector so as not to leave them without work (in the absence of unemployment benefit). This meant traditional overemployment in the southern regions of Italy (Interv. *Ceriani*).

3. Subsidiarity is not only a regional model, but at local level it is also an important driving principle (Interv. *Rovati*). It is also an interesting idea at national level, and so in the Italian Parliament an interparty group of two hundred members has been formed to deal with this principle (Interv. *Vittadini*).

4. In Europe, how to maintain the welfare state with fewer financial resources but with growing needs from the population is a common problem. Is it possible to restrict the health service to no more than a proportion of society in Europe? If not, then a solution could be the subsidiarity model (Interv. *Vittadini*).

5. For example, LegaCoop, Confederazione delle Cooperative, Acli, Compagnia delle Opere (CdO non profit), Movi (Movimento Volontariato Italiano) Caritas Lombardia, Gruppi di Volontariato Vincenziano, Società san Vincenzo de Paoli.
6. The current economic crises further deepen the problem of redistribution. The Lombardy regional budget should also be cut, and this means an opportunity to better tailor policy interventions and to simplify the procedures.
7. The data set of the study only focuses on the current expenditure and the year 2005. The authors neglected interest payments on public debt and taxes moving across regions.

## References

Ambrosanio, M. F., M. Bordignon, and F. Cerniglia (2010) "Constitutional reforms, fiscal decentralization and regional fiscal flows in Italy" in N. Bosch, M. Espasa, and A. Solé-Ollé (eds.), *Political Economy of Interregional Fiscal Flows* (Cheltenham: Elgar), 75–107.

Armajani, B. (2009) "Subsidiarity and research: Means for the new challenges" in IReR, *Punti di vista. Lombardia 2010* (Milan: Guerini), 10.

Brugnoli, A., and G. Vittadini (2009) *Subsidiarity: Positive Anthropology and Social Organization. Foundations for a New Conception of State and Market and Key Points of the Experience in Lombardy* (Milan: Guerini).

Colombo, A. (2008) "The 'Lombardy model': Subsidiarity-informed regional governance" in *Social Policy & Administration*, 42(2), 177–96.

Colombo, A., and M. Mazzoleni (2007) "Innovating policies and government in an Italian region. Lombardy's model of governance" in A. Brugnoli, A. Colombo, and M. Mazzoleni (eds.), *Governance: The Lombardy Way. Assessing an Experience, Designing New Perspectives* (Milan: Guerini) 53–84.

Hopkins, J. W. (2002) *Devolution in Context: Regional, Federal and Devolved Government in the European Union* (London-Sydney: Cavendish), 101–14.

Horváth, Gy. (1993) "Regionalism and devolution in the dual Italy." Manuscript.

IReR (2009a) *Indagine su enti di ricerca che supportano i governi regionali nel mondo* (Milan).

IReR (2009b) *Lombardy Region. Economic and Institutional Features, an Experience in Government* (Unpublished) (Milan).

Keating, M. (1997) "The invention of regions: Political restructuring and territorial government in Western Europe" in *Environment and Planning C: Government and Policy*, 15, 383–98.

Kitson, M. (2009) "Local responses to global changes" in IReR, *Punti di vista. Lombardia 2010* (Milan: Guerini), 78–79.

Le Grand, J. (2003) *Motivation, Agency and Public Policy: Of Knights and Knaves, Pawns and Queens* (Oxford: Oxford University Press).

Le Grand, J. (2007) *The Other Invisible Hand. Delivering Public Services through Choice and Competition* (Princeton-Oxford: Princeton University Press).

Leadbeater, C. (2009) "Lombardy: A state of relationships" in IReR, *Punti di vista. Lombardia 2010* (Milan: Guerini), 80–81.

Leicht, K. T., and J. C. Jenkins (eds.) (2010) *Handbook of Politics. State and Society in Global Perspectives* (New York and London: Springer).

Lowery, D. (1998) "Consumer sovereignty and quasi-market failure" in *Journal of Public Administration Research & Theory*, 2, 137–72.

Migdal, J. S. (2004) *State in Society* (Cambridge: Cambridge University Press).

Mussati, G. (1993) "The development of the Lombardy region" in Gy. Horváth (ed.), *Development Strategies in the Alpine-Adriatic Region* (Pécs: Centre for Regional Studies Hungarian Academy of Sciences) 83–107.

Powell, M. (2003) "Quasi-markets in British health policy: A Longue Durée perspective" in *Social Policy & Administration*, 7, 725–41.

Powell, M. (2007) *The 'Horizontal' Dimension: Decentralisation, Partnership and Governance of Welfare*. June 1, 2007. Available on IReR website, http://www.irer.it/eventi/governancerelazionigiugno2007/Powellrelazione.pdf, accessed on October 4, 2011.

Sellers, J. M. (2010) "State-society relations beyond the Weberian state" in M. Bevir (ed.), *Handbook of Governance* (London: Sage Publications). Available at http://www.usc.edu/dept/polsci/sellers/Publications/Assets/State%20Society%20Relations%20JMS%2020090731.pdf, accessed on October 4, 2011.

# 5

# A VIEW FROM THE ANTIPODES: COMPARING THE LOMBARD AND NEW ZEALAND WAYS OF GOVERNANCE

*Philip McDermott*

## 5.1. INTRODUCTION

This chapter reviews the Lombard model of governance from a New Zealand perspective.

Regional government in Lombardy observes the principle of vertical subsidiarity through which decisions should be made at the level of government closest to its citizens in order to "include individuals in decisions relating to the exercise of public power" (Colombo and O'Sullivan, 2012, p. 4), subject to the competence of the relevant agency. More than this, Lombardy's governance is distinctive in pursuing horizontal as well as vertical subsidiarity. This provides for the inclusion of nongovernmental organizations—civil society—in the development and delivery of public services.

In New Zealand a period of significant local government reform began in 1989. The original aims were rationalization of a system that had become cumbersome, the pursuit of cost efficiencies, and improved decision making. The reforms also promised a degree of decentralization in what had become at a highly centralized system of government underpinned by an overcomplex and fragmented array of statutory agencies for local service development and delivery.

Ongoing reforms have sought to reconcile the pursuit of efficiency in local services with local democracy. Emphasis on formalizing consultative processes as a way to legitimize decisions made by elected representatives reflects central government's concerns over the performance of local government and a preference for a managerial approach to governance rather than a commitment to devolution.

The aim has been for improved consultation to increase the transparency and accountability of council decisions and programs.

Consequently, subsidiarity as such has not featured in the New Zealand reforms. However, the notion that more effective local government might provide some balance to the "unbridled power" of central government has played a small role (Palmer, 1995), and the possible scope of local government activity has been widened.

Significant differences in history, context, and scale condition the comparison of local governance between Italy and New Zealand. One key difference is the centrality of the notion of citizenship and particularly membership of the European Union in shaping the rights and obligations of individuals in Italy. Membership of free trade agreements and a close economic association with Australia raise no such issues for New Zealand citizens. Here, however, the question of the rights of indigenous people does cut across debates about citizens' and institutions' rights and obligations.

Despite these differences, common concerns for boosting efficiency and local empowerment are common to New Zealand and Lombardy mainly as a means of holding councils to account in the former and as a means of enhancing program delivery in the latter. On these grounds, the quite different heritage of local government in New Zealand provides a useful benchmark for assessment of elements of the Lombard model of local governance.

## 5.2. THE PRINCIPLES AND PRACTICE OF SUBSIDIARITY

Subsidiarity involves allocation of responsibilities for governing from central to decentralized agencies on the grounds that decisions are best taken as close as possible to where they will have the most effect.

However, in constitutional terms the principle behind subsidiarity is the converse of this downward delegation. Through subsidiarity centralized authority is subordinated to decentralized authority as it is communities of citizens that confer powers on governments to act on their behalf. This principle of subordination of central to local authority simply acknowledges that some actions are better taken at higher levels than lower levels for technical and efficiency reasons.

As a guiding principle for good government, subsidiarity has strong underpinnings in the literature of political philosophy (IReR, 2009). Among other things, it has played an important role in the formation of the nation-state when quasi-independent provinces have transferred power to a collective authority formed to serve the common good, giving rise to the federal state. There is a paradox, though, as centralized government in turn assumes authority over its sponsors:

> Whether there ought to be a federal government entrusted with the care of the common defense is a question in the first instance open to discussion; but the moment it is decided in the affirmative, it will follow that government ought to be clothed with all the powers requisite to complete execution of its trust. (Hamilton, 1788, p. 23)

This duality of authority can lead to tensions between a nation-state and its parts. Ideally, this is resolved through a constitution that enables powers to be allocated with some clarity and creates a role for judicial interpretation when disputes arise.

The principles underlying subsidiarity may—or should—play a major role in determining the transfer of powers from the lower to the higher authority. In practice, this may lead to a reluctant concession of power by members—states, regions, or provinces—to the federal government, with the result that citizens become further removed from the authority in public matters.

French politician-philosopher Proudhon addressed this conflict in the mid-nineteenth century by suggesting a division between responsibilities for the powers of legislation and delivery:

> Only the contract of federation, whose essence is that of serving more and more to the citizens than the State, to the municipal and provincial authorities than to the central authority, could put us on the road to truth. In a free society the role of the State or the government is par excellence a role of legislation, institution, creation, inauguration, installation, that is as little as possible a role of execution. (Proudhon, cited in IReR, 2009, p. 36)

This distinction lies in the division between central regulation—the setting of standards and development of institutions spanning the interests of the constituent parts—and local execution. It is founded on the notion that the state is empowered by—and the servant of—its citizens.

Not only does the principle of subsidiarity help determine the appropriate level for policy formation or for action (vertical subsidiarity), it also helps determine the appropriate agency for policy delivery (horizontal subsidiarity). It may be the pursuit of horizontal subsidiarity that makes the vertical subsidiarity through which the region of Lombardy exercises its authority so effective.

## 5.2.1. Subsidiarity, Federation, and the Emergence of New Nations

Federation was the process through which the colonial settlements of the North America and Australia were transformed into nation-states, forming central governments and assigning to them responsibility for such tasks as foreign affairs, defense, public order and justice, currency and trade.

### 5.2.1.1. The United States of America

The Articles of Confederation were drafted in 1776 and 1777 following the Declaration of Independence by the Second National Congress of States. The aim was the collective freedom, sovereignty, and independence of the United States. After ratification in 1781 they became the first constitution of the United States of America, providing for the central government to conduct diplomacy and make war.

The subsequent Constitution of 1788 was prepared by state representatives and ratified by the legislatures of the thirteen individual states making up the Congress of Confederation. It provided the structures for national legislative, executive, and judicial powers; defined the powers of the federal government; and established the relationships among states and between states and the federal government. Through Article 6 of the Constitution the states also ratified the supremacy of federal over state law.

However, state governments retain inherent powers to act unless limited by the state or federal constitution. They retain significant responsibilities, including education, public health, safety, policing, and selected areas of law. States also share some functions with the federal government, including legislation and courts, highways, welfare, and finance (borrowing and taxation).

States confer authority upward to the federal government and delegate it downward to local government. Many state functions are administered by local government, an arrangement dating back to the colonies, although the structure and functions of local government vary among states. Local government includes counties, cities, towns, boroughs, and villages, and some consolidated variants.

The number of small democratic institutions for local service delivery and multiple tiers of local government reflect a strongly democratic tradition with a wide range of officers chosen through the ballot box. Groups of local councils may also form regional associations for collaboration and coordination of services, but not at the cost of the power of individual members.

### 5.2.1.2. Canada

The Canadian Federation formed in 1867 comprised the erstwhile British Province of Canada divided into the two new provinces of Ontario and Quebec and two other British colonies, New Brunswick and Nova Scotia. The British Colonial Office recognized the Dominion of Canada as a self-governing colony. In this way, legitimacy was conferred from below, by federation, and from above by recognition by Britain.

Canada comprises thirteen provinces and territories. Federal functions are defined, in part, as the residual of functions not granted by constitution to the provinces. They include trade and commerce, navigation and shipping, fisheries, Indian relations, criminal law, and international treaties.

Provincial governments deal with health care, education, transport, property, and civil rights. Again, local government acts largely as an agency of the provinces, and subject to their control. Local government functions are generally defined with reference to the needs of local communities and land use, covering planning, development and transport, utility services, parks, local policing and fire fighting, local welfare services, recreation, and culture.

Local government also deals directly with the federal government, which may fund local infrastructure and may help to implement centrally funded welfare programs.

### 5.2.1.3. Australia

Six self-governing British colonies formed the Australian Commonwealth through federation in 1901. This was in response to increasing physical and economic integration as a result of improving transport, communication, and trade links among them. It followed the earlier establishment of a Federal Council of Australasia (1888), comprising Queensland, Tasmania, Victoria, Western Australia, and Fiji. This earlier, loose federation was intended to promote trade through regularizing tariffs and standardizing transport, and to develop a joint position in response to concerns about the growing German and French presence in the South Pacific.

In Australia the Commonwealth government is responsible for taxation, defense, foreign affairs, and postal and telecommunication services. The states retain power over all other matters within their borders, including police, hospitals, education, and public transport. However, where conflicts in law arise, the Constitution provides for commonwealth to prevail over state law.

Local government is not provided for in the federal constitution but set out in state constitutions. Local responsibilities vary between states. In any case, local government functions are limited given the wide scope of state action. They tend to deal with planning and development, local parks, solid and liquid waste management, and public facilities.

### 5.2.1.4. New Zealand

New Zealand differs from the three federal states described above. Britain annexed New Zealand in 1840 to establish the rule of law, in part to protect indigenous Māori against the lawlessness of settlers (whalers, seal hunters, and the like). The key instrument of annexation was the Treaty of Waitangi, an agreement signed by British Crown representative and a majority—but not all—chiefs of the many Māori tribes who occupied the country.

The 1840 Treaty is considered by many to be the founding document of the nation. By signing it indigenous Māori of different tribes collectively ceded powers best exercised centrally to Britain. This contrasted with federation elsewhere, through which powers were ceded to an agency of the colonists' own making. The Māori interest was in protection of their customary rights by the Crown in the face of growing pressure on land and resources from European settlers.

Ambiguity in the translation of the Treaty and differences in the meanings of the Māori- and English-language versions and in the expectations of the signatories mean that it remains contested. It is a focus for grievances on the part of Māori over the loss of rights and resources (Kawharau, 1989). This perennial issue is behind a constitutional review announced by the deputy prime minister and minister of māori affairs in late 2010. It was highlighted by an earlier review that commented:

> The issues surrounding the constitutional impact of the Treaty are so unclear, contested, and socially significant, that it seems likely that anything but the most minor and technical constitutional change would require deliberate effort to engage with hapū and iwi [sub-tribal social and organizing units] as part of the process of public debate. (Constitutional Arrangements Committee, 2005)

Despite its inherent ambiguity, the Treaty of Waitangi remains a significant constitutional check on the power of central government (Palmer and Palmer, 2004) and in this respect might be considered to embody an element of subsidiarity.

As in other colonies, European occupation of New Zealand took place in several widely dispersed coastal settlements. However, the signing of a treaty effectively covering the whole country meant that formal federation was not a prerequisite to nationhood. Instead, a Royal Charter prepared in Britain provided for the division of New Zealand into administrative divisions with local bodies to oversee local services, policing, and justice.

The British Constitution Act of 1852 created a General Assembly and provided for six provinces. While the Act preempted federation and limited their powers, provincial councils became active ahead of the General Assembly and so initially took control of wide range of functions, leaving relations with Māori as the principal General Assembly function.

Eventually limited resources and infighting among provincial councils led the General Assembly to assert its powers, abolishing them in 1876. The result was two-tier government with the role of local government prescribed by the center.

As a result local government in New Zealand is controlled directly by central statute. Governments of all shades have been conservative when it comes to delegating powers or functions to local councils. Consequently, local government has not acted as a check on central government, as might be expected in a two-tier system, nor has its obviously empowered local communities. Rather, it has played a purely instrumental part in governance. As discussed below, this is changing. However, it is fair to say that in a setting in which subsidiarity has played only a limited constitutional role change has been more about form and performance than function or philosophy.

## 5.3. The Lombard Model

According to Colombo (2008, p. 182), growing recourse to the notion of subsidiarity in the European context is constrained, being used as a "political/legal instrument to define competences between the EU and member states only." This is *vertical* subsidiarity, confined to the division of responsibilities among different layers within the public sphere.

This contrasts with horizontal subsidiarity, which "relates to the sharing of competences and initiatives between public and private actors" (Colombo, 2008, p. 182). Horizontal subsidiarity draws on the Pope Pius XI 1931 Encyclical Letter, designed to offset the reduction of intermediary powers between the individual and the state resulting from the rise of individualism and the decline of social life.

The appropriation by the state of functions that could be performed by "lesser groups" is seen to limit individual freedoms. It may also reduce the effectiveness of the state by distracting it from roles for which it is best suited.

Subsidiarity can be interpreted as form of social organization that moves along a vertical dimension from central to regional to local scope, and along a horizontal dimension from individual to group and ultimately institutionalized action. The role of government is to entrust private agents of various sorts (such as nonprofit organizations) to exercise public good functions.

> According to this logic, the primacy in implementing public policies should be assigned through contractual relationship to third sector actors [...with] an explicit ethical mission [...] a strong sharing of objectives, organizational integration based on the sharing of common values, a low vertical and horizontal specialization [and] a leadership based on charisma, and a strong vocation to operate in a network. (Lippi and Morisi, 2005, p. 74; cited in Colombo, 2008, p. 185)

This model of subsidiarity depends on a highly developed civil society and a governance philosophy that affords it a significant place. There are parallels with the Third Way and its emphasis on personal responsibility Giddens (1998) and with associative democracy through devolution of as many of the functions of state as possible to civil society (Hirst and Bader, 2001).

Finally, Colombo links subsidiarity to the notion of social reciprocity, informing relations on the basis of the mutual fulfillment of participants, distinguishing between the *contract* defining one-off market transactions and the *compact* based on developing ongoing relationships among participants.

### 5.3.1. Implementation: State-Region Relations

The Lombard model of governance has been developed since the mid-1990s through institutional reforms derived from the concept of subsidiarity and "characterised by the central importance given to the capabilities and contribution of individuals, families and social groups and by its commitment to the regulatory role of the State" (Colombo and O'Sullivan, 2012, p. 1).

The 1990s saw a strengthening of the power of the regions within Italy's federal state by granting of additional areas of competence and revenue streams. In 1999, regions assumed control over their own statutes, electoral systems, and forms of government. The "Title V reform" of 2001 "restored" or strengthened subsidiarity as it did the following:

1. Abolished the constitutional superiority of the state over local authorities;
2. Defined the field of exclusive national or state competence to include foreign and EU affairs, immigration, religious affairs, and the protection of basic civil and social rights;
3. Defined areas of shared competence, including the international relations of regions, education, research, and health;
4. Defined policy areas not allocated as areas of regional competence;
5. Allowed for central government to impinge on regional competence "only in order to preserve national unity and security, basic civil and social rights, and international and EU law." (Colombo, 2008, p. 180)

Colombo and O'Sullivan outline a number of constraints on regional autonomy. The first is the persistence of centralist structures and decision making, especially on expenditure. State institutions remain dominant: central government staff outnumbers regional Lombard staff by 8:1.

The second is the long-standing institutional form, values, and norms of federal government. These support more rigid and comprehensive regulation than appropriate for the delegation implied in subsidiarity, and limit the fiscal capacity of regions to fulfil their notional competencies.

The third constraint is the overbearing impact on regions of having to manage the health-care sector and the disproportionate demands it makes on regional budgets.

Finally, the authors hold that the geographic redistribution of taxes by the federal government has become unbalanced so that "not only is it rather unsustainable, but it is also increasingly perceived as both an unjust burden for some regions and as a waste of resources" (Colombo and O'Sullivan, 2012, p. 3).

### 5.3.2. Implementation: The Lombard Model

While the strength of national government may limit the scope of regional action, it is the way in which the Lombardy Regional Government has chosen to exercise its authority that makes its governance distinctive. According to Colombo and O'Sullivan, the regional government's strategic role ensures "that services are delivered in the best interests of taxpayers and users" and upholds "procedures designed to maintain local influence and accountability."

The capacity of the regional government to deliver services traditionally provided by central government is strengthened by drawing on the resources of civil society. Indeed, the decentralized delivery that accompanies subsidiarity may prove more effective and efficient for some services than a centralized model, even though public resources appear more thinly spread.

The "From Government to Governance" policy is concerned with openness and participation; monitoring and control; regulating systems of services; and informing the management of policy, but not the mechanics of delivery. In some areas regional government maintains planning, regulatory, and financial roles only, devolving management and delivery to autonomous bodies (Colombo and O'Sullivan, 2012, p. 5). Three operating principles underpin this movement:

1. The *pluralism of providers*, separating planning from delivery and avoiding dominance by monopolies and oligopolies by allowing for delivery by private and nonprofit organizations;
2. *Freedom of choice* that allows citizens to choose a provider through, for example, voucher systems, informed by supplier accreditation and evaluation;
3. *Fiscal subsidiarity* aimed at a distribution of public resources to sustain both service demand and supply.

In several policy areas: "the regional government has opted to keep in its hands only the functions of regulating, programming and financing, while the management and delivery of services has been devolved to autonomous bodies, either public or private, so that government administration does not intervene in those fields where society is able to effectively carry out public functions" (Colombo, 2008, p.188).

Regional government plays the role of "rule maker" maximizing the choices available to citizens. For example, in welfare services the region funds projects that are presented by families' associations through an annual tender. It also provides vouchers so that families can choose between public and private providers for the care of the elderly and disabled (Colombo, 2008, pp.188–89).

Families can also be subsidized to send children to private schools, making it easier for more to choose them. In health, the region has shifted from being a monopoly service provider to focus on strategy, regulation, and finance, with local health agencies organizing service delivery sensitive to local needs through private and public providers, lifting standards and choice (Colombo, 2008, p. 189).

The Lombard project is ongoing. Among the challenges are the need for independent, transparent, and effective auditing of the areas subject to reform; considering the possible role of a market model; fiscal challenges; and overcoming the inertia associated with a long-standing tradition of passive welfare assistance.

Colombo concluded that the "historical legacy of a centralized Napoleonic *Rechsstaat* has meant that the early policy outcomes of the [Lombard] model often bear a distinct affinity with strategies of public service liberalization 'for efficiency's sake' pursued elsewhere." However, given its ideological foundation, future initiatives under the Lombard model "are likely to differ significantly from those derived from a neo-liberal agenda" (Colombo, 2008, pp.193).

Subsidiarity is, thus, more than a tool for structuring government. It provides the moral authority for a particular style of governance. It does not predetermine where functions should lie, but provides principles to help communities make that determination.

Vertical subsidiarity has become an important guiding principle in Italy for regional government and its relationship with central government. Lombardy has embraced horizontal subsidiarity to take advantage of the resulting delegations. This is a "work in progress," however. There are constitutional constraints on how far it can act with authority in a number of areas (central government remaining the dominant player), and how it might increase its capacity and influence in others. Horizontal subsidiarity, leveraging off a range of civil society suppliers, offers an important prospect for overcoming constraints. Continuing to build the capacity of civil society and lift its commitment to regional programs is a promising direction and should help reduce the risk of confusing the application of subsidiarity to local and regional affairs with a neoliberal agenda of reducing the role of government generally.

The experience of the other nations considered here raises another prospect: how far might subsidiarity be pursued by promoting the role of *local* government. This implies a shift from the situation in which local government is no more than an agent of state or provincial government. The experience in New Zealand following twenty years of reform of local government may cast some light on this prospect.

## 5.4. Local Government Reform in New Zealand

### 5.4.1. The Setting

In global terms, New Zealand is remote, comprising two main islands 2,000 km east of Australia in the Southwest Pacific.

Over 85 percent of New Zealanders reside in urban settlements, the majority in fertile coastal plains separated by mountainous terrain or hill country. Auckland in the north of the North Island is the primate city, with one-third of the country's population (1.4 million). Wellington region, which houses the capital city at the southern end of the North Island, has fewer than 480,000 people. Christchurch, the largest city in the South Island, has 370,000.

### 5.4.2. New Zealand's Government

New Zealand has a unitary system of government with a house of representatives comprising 120 members voted on a proportional representation basis (through a mix of constituent and list seats), including seven seats reserved for voters of Māori ethnicity. Executive power resides in a cabinet of ministers selected by the prime minister who is the parliamentary leader of the majority party. Elections are held every three years based on mixed member proportional representation. The government is most likely to be made up of an alliance of parties, with the prime minister being the leader of the majority partner.

Local government is empowered by statute. Its powers have traditionally been distinctly fewer than in some other countries. For example, health, police, and education are run by central government.

Local government representatives are elected directly by ward. Although mayors are elected at large the New Zealand model is that of a weak mayor, where the executive authority rests within the council rather than the office of mayor.

There are also fifteen regional councils, again with members elected directly by ward. Regional council chairmen, though, are elected by the representatives themselves and so do not embody the popular leadership associated with a mayor.

Regional and local councils are differentiated by function rather than by subordination of one to the other. Regional government is responsible for cross-boundary functions—particularly water, air, and soil (relating to erosion) quality, and pest (weeds, wildlife) management. It is also responsible for public transport, transport planning, and civil defense.

The seventy-four local authorities (cities and districts) are traditionally responsible for land use, public health, water supply, local roads, waste disposal, parks and reserves, recreational and community infrastructure. Under the Local Government Act 2002 they were granted powers of general competence but have tended not to deviate far from their traditional roles.

The potential for regional councils spanning metropolitan areas to broaden their functions has seen some conflict as they have become more directly involved in land use regulation, technically the responsibility of city and district councils, to help fulfill their environmental and transport mandates. The resulting confusion of governance was one of the factors behind the recent creation of a unitary council for Auckland Region (see below).

Community boards are directly elected to represent community interests within each local council area. Their influence is limited, though, to functions delegated by local councils.

### 5.4.3. Subsidiarity in New Zealand

In New Zealand subsidiarity can be considered at two levels.

First, it is relevant to a formal commitment made in 1979 to Closer Economic Relations between New Zealand and Australia. There have been continuing initiatives to align business between the two nations (creating a single market) on the back of long-standing freedom of movement of citizens. Aligning economic regulation is not yet complete, though, and those areas traditionally associated with subsidiarity at the highest level—defense, foreign affairs, and currency—remain independent (although subject to some cooperation).

There is no equivalent behind Closer Economic Relations to the role of subsidiarity in maintaining the freedom of people to relocate across EU borders and to conduct transnational business without undue impediment in the European Community. The application of subsidiarity at this level is perhaps constrained by New Zealand's inability to influence trans-Tasman outcomes when the Australian position will often have to be reconciled across the six states as well as agreed at the transnational level (Guerin, 2002, p. 4).

Second, subsidiarity is implicit in the restructuring of local government since the 1980s, but has had little obvious influence. There has been debate about the appropriate allocation of functions *to* government and *between* central and local government. However, restructuring has been driven in large part by an agenda of reducing government rather than devolving or delegating public responsibilities. Debate is framed in terms of economic efficiency and shaped by the radical managerial reform of central government that took place from 1984 onward. Through this a monetarist economic policy displaced a tradition of Keynesianism, and a legacy of a developmental and paternalistic government gave way to a more minimalist approach (Kelsey, 1995; Easton, 1997).

### 5.4.4. The 1989 Local Government Reforms

Local government reforms commenced in 1989. Yet, despite promotion of the principle of subsidiarity by a Royal Commission on Social Policy the year earlier (Royal Commission on Social Policy, 1988, p. 806), changes in the form and role of local government were driven almost entirely by economic theories. The rights of the citizen have only been advanced in a secondary discourse based on democratic theory, without obvious recourse to the principles of subsidiarity.

Public sector reform in general was "concerned with agency theory and New Institutional Economic theory" (Reid, 1999, p. 179). The former is concerned with aligning interests through the information shared and contract established between principal and subordinate. The latter is concerned with costs associated with how institutions are structured and operate. Both sit within a neoclassical framework focusing on cost reduction.

Indeed, early thinking by central government officials turned subsidiarity on its head, suggesting that local government should only be used where national delivery of public services was not possible. The underlying presumption was that centralized services are intrinsically more efficient than decentralized services (Officials Coordinating Committee on Local Government, 1988). At an institutional level (in the critical sense; see, e.g., Hodgson, 2006) this reflects a long-standing distrust on the part of the center regarding the capacity of local government (Reid, 1999, p. 167).

Issues of competence do impact local government performance. Despite a sparse population, by 1988 there were 829 local government bodies: 217 territorial authorities (city, borough, town, and district councils), 136 community councils (elected advisory boards), 23 regional councils (mainly coordinating local councils), and 453 single purpose (or ad hoc) authorities.

The latter covered such diverse activities as airports, river catchments, education, electricity distribution, hospitals, economic development, liquor licensing, maritime planning, harbor management, and so forth. Their powers were prescribed through legislation. Their proliferation over the century following abolition of the provinces reinforced the dominance of central government because the many, small, single purpose units depended on it for their legitimacy and funding.

The overall result was a crowded, confused, and inefficient domain of authorities. The often very small scale and single functions of ad hoc government agencies meant management and production efficiencies were difficult to come by, while any sense of democracy was impaired by the very low level of voter turnout and lack of knowledge about who candidates were and what they stood for.

The 1989 local government reforms followed the managerial model of transformation of central government that preceded it (Howell et al., 1996, p. 26). This had dealt with increasing competition by dismantling support for production (import quotas, tariffs, and subsidies); withdrawal of government from commercial or quasi-commercial activities through sales to the private sector and the creation of state-owned enterprises for government-owned trading functions; and separating policy development, regulation, and service delivery in the interests of a more transparent and accountable government.

The second two streams were applied to local government through structural change and a "purchaser-supplier" model for services. City and district councils were also required to withdraw from commercial or quasi-commercial operations, and establish Local Area Trading Enterprises for such commercial assets as remained in public ownership, including ports, airports, electricity distribution, and public transport. Alternative governance models were allowed for more traditional infrastructure, such as water supply and wastewater management.

Transparency was increased by separating regulation from service delivery, publication of annual plans and reports, and adopting new financial standards (in 1996). The latter included ten-year budgets and accrual accounting to better identify the commitment of resources by activity and enable performance to be monitored. The resulting increase in transparency was expected to lift the standard of public decision making.

No functional change of significance was incorporated into the 1989 reforms. Local government duties continued to be prescribed by central legislation. The reforms were driven by a managerial more than democratic agenda, with the emphasis on structural changes. In theory, stronger local government should have been able to assume more responsibilities locally to support a leaner central government. However, while spending by local government expended over the 1990s, and central government spending contracted slightly, this did not reflect any significant realignment of functions.[1]

One of the architects of the reforms, Local Government Commissioner Brian Elwood, argued that in terms of local democracy:

> What is important is not so much that thousands [of citizens] within each local area could participate but don't, but the obligation upon councils to operate in a way that provides an opportunity for participation keeps the system functioning in an open manner and is at all times capable of being brought to account. (Elwood, 1995)

This theme—that the *opportunity* for citizens to participate in democratic processes legitimizes local government actions—has become an important prop to local government reform in New Zealand.

Given the legitimacy conferred by an increased capacity for participation Elwood concluded:

> Councils are freer than before to undertake the assumption of leadership and facilitation role and to make decisions based on justification, efficiency and common sense, rather than some prescriptive legislation. (McDermott, 1995, p. 17)

Elwood saw the reform of local government's funding base from reliance on property taxes to greater dependence on user payments as an outstanding reform issue that needed to happen to increase the local autonomy he saw as implicit in the 1989 reforms (Elwood, 1995, p. 315). The market logic is more immediate, though, presuming that citizens will rationalize consumption of public services if faced directly with the cost of supply.

The favored change in the funding model leans toward a neoliberal interpretation of subsidiarity, whereby consumer preferences prevail through individual market decisions. This privileges individuals in the market rather than individuals acting in civil society, the foundation of subsidiarity in political philosophy, and illustrates the fine line between purely economic and purely social expectations of what subsidiarity might deliver.

Within New Zealand there has been a shift in the direction of more market mechanisms influencing the supply of erstwhile public goods. Despite this, issues around costs and funding continue to undermine citizen and central government confidence in local government (Shand et al., 2007).

Howell et al. argued that despite the 1989 reforms New Zealand retained a weak form of local government, a legacy of the abolition of provinces over a century earlier. This reflected the separation of significant social responsibilities from multi-purpose local government, an overcentralized system for managing health, education and welfare functions, and confused accountabilities, due in part to funding anomalies. There are still too many territorial units which do not correspond with the physical, economic, and social boundaries of communities. (Howell et al., 1996, p. 60)

### 5.4.5. The Local Government Act 2002

Further reform occurred in 2002 when a center-left government sought to simplify the empowering legislation. Local democracy did feature in this round of reform, although cost reduction still played a part. The overall aim was to empower local government, enabling it to respond with greater flexibility to the needs of an increasingly diverse society (Reid, 2001).

The result was a complete rewrite of the local government legislation, removing the prescription of functions and conferring the power of general competence on councils. This was accompanied by a statement of local government responsibility for community "well-being." The new act also detailed consultation and reporting procedures to help increase community influence over decision making.

The 2002 Act replaced functional prescription with procedural requirements, including the following:

1. Guidance emphasizing openness, consultation, and accountability, promoting a community-focused mandate (Part 2, 14; see Appendix);
2. Governance structures and processes that are "effective open and transparent" and separation of regulatory from non-regulatory processes (Part 4, 39);
3. The publication of governance statements covering functions, responsibilities, electoral arrangements, representation arrangements, members' roles, meeting processes, and consultation policies, including policies for liaising with Māori (Part 4, 40);
4. The establishment of community boards to: represent the interests of their communities, consider matters referred to them by the council; provide an overview of council services; provide annual submissions on expenditure; communicate with local organizations; and undertake other responsibilities delegated by the council;
5. The establishment of "Council-controlled organizations" (corporatization) to undertake some local authority functions (Part 5);

6. A policy on matters the council considers significant (proportionality) as a basis for determining appropriate consultation procedures.

The Act details decision-making procedures including identification of options, analysis, consultation (including particular provision for input by Māori), and justification for decisions.

### 5.4.6. Planning for Community Outcomes

Under the Local Government Act 2002 local authorities are required to "identify community outcomes for the intermediate and long-term future of its district or region" in order to

1. Provide opportunities to discuss desired outcomes in terms of the present and future, social, economic, environmental, and cultural well-being of the communities;
2. Allow communities to discuss the relative importance and priorities of identified outcomes to the present and future social, economic, and environmental well-being of the community;
3. Provide scope to measure progress toward the achievement of community outcomes; and
4. Inform and guide the setting of priorities in relation to the activities of the local authority and other organizations.

The (ten-year) long-term council community plan is required to:

1. Describe the activities of the council;
2. Describe the anticipated community outcomes for the district or region;
3. Provide for integrated decision making and coordination of resources;
4. Provide a long-term focus for the decisions and activities of the local authority;
5. Provide a basis for accountability of the local authority in the community; and
6. Provide an opportunity for participation by the public in decision-making processes on activities to be undertaken by the local authority (Part 6, 93).

Implementation is fine-tuned through an annual plan and budget that demonstrate how the outcomes defined in the long-term council community plan are being pursued, with performance reviewed in an annual report.

### 5.4.7. Results So Far

The national Audit Office review of the 2009–2019 plans concluded that councils have made progress in long-term planning and monitoring, but that there is room for improved asset management, service monitoring, and financial strategies (Controller and Auditor General, 2010).

The focus of performance evaluation remains on fiscal matters, and how efficiently councils deliver the services that the community seeks from them. The Audit Office was concerned that a financial strategy "should be presented to the community as a major issue" because it "most significantly determines the future state, both for the financial and consequently service delivery ability, of the local authority" (Controller and Auditor General, 2010, p. 15).

The Office emphasized the fiscal gains that should be available to councils through long-term planning, rather than on how far the new focus on community outcomes may have shifted priorities to match local needs. Yet, it is the latter more than the former that would mark real gains in local democracy resulting from a more consultative approach.

The Department of Internal Affairs—responsible for oversight of the Local Government Act—also reviewed councils' long-term council community plans. It too focused on financial aspects, concentrating on shifts in costs and revenue streams (Department of Internal Affairs, 2009).

Neither the Department of Internal Affairs nor the Audit Office analyzed possible changes in the roles and spending of councils of the sort that might be expected in response to signals from their communities regarding local priorities. Having given councils the tools to enable them to realign programs with community priorities, the government has yet to examine how far this has happened.

An independent review of the 2002 Act suggests that competing views of local government's role—minimalist and activist—have acted against the emergence of a coherent strategy for the sector (Hewison, 2009). Hewison cited the European Charter of Local Self-Government, 1985 as a useful precedent. Indeed, he suggests that in a globalized world New Zealand may have little option but to adopt such a charter so that it can comply with international standards, in much the same way as international human rights, environmental, phyto-sanitary, and health standards might be adopted as a condition of participation in international commerce.

Hewison suggests that individual councils could choose to adopt the principles of the European Charter even if the country does not. He proposes that the purpose of local government, 2002 could be extended in the Local Government Act to include the principles of local self-government set out in the Charter.

In what seems like a variant on the principle of subsidiarity, it was expected that the reforms brought about by the 2002 Act would place local government in a better position to form partnerships with central government to work jointly toward community objectives. However, given the multiplicity of departments and statues through which central government deals with the many issues that influence local well-being, it has been difficult for local and central government to align their programs. The best that has been managed is an annual forum between the two to discuss matters of common interest.

Hewison cites a number of precedents for formalizing the central-local relationship, including an agreement between the state and local government in South Australia. In Canada, the relationship between regional districts and the province of British Columbia is set out in the Local Government Act, Chapter 323 (British Columbia), which he suggests could be incorporated in some form or another into the New Zealand Act. Failing central government interest, he again suggests this could be an initiative for individual councils to pursue.

Finally, Hewison considers how far the Local Government Act 2002 clarified the relationship with Māori. It commits councils to establishing and maintaining processes that enable Māori to contribute to its decision making (Section 81). While according to Hewison this "contains very extensive obligations for local authorities" and is far-reaching in terms of Māori well-being, the Act still leaves it to the discretion of each council to determine how it might do these things.

Hewison concludes that the relationship between local government and Māori will be an evolving one, which is at least promoted and fostered, if not resolved, by the provisions of the Local Government Act 2002.

### 5.4.7. The Implications for Subsidiarity

The rewriting of the Local Government Act in 2002 represented a substantial shift of principle, from one whereby councils could only do what they were empowered to do by central statute, to one whereby they could undertake any function subject to a community mandate verified through consultation. In theory, this changed the relationship between central and local government. Yet, there has been no transfer of powers as a result. Instead, the emphasis has been on promoting fiscal and reporting standards first and foremost

The requirement is for councils to be seen to consult. Progress in terms of vertical subsidiarity is weak, though. Central government has not noticeably relinquished functions, despite the view that "in a number of respects the consultation, planning, and accountability practices of local authorities are more advanced than those of central government" (Shand et al., 2007, p. 3).

Equally, few councils have delegated powers to local boards (although there are exceptions).

The potential for greater horizontal subsidiarity also exists through partnerships with central government and greater freedom to engage private sector agencies. There is some increased consultation in economic and social matters, but there is no evidence that central government has embraced the idea that local agencies may be better placed to deal with such issues than it is.

In fact, central government established a "satellite" Auckland Policy Office in 2005 (formerly the Government Urban and Economic Development Office) to better align its interdepartmental priorities for the region, the role being "developing and implementing government policy in Auckland." While it has worked with local government in research and policy, the office perhaps reflects a long-standing distrust of local government through an increased central government presence in Auckland.

Despite its genesis in a desire to create more effective local government through open decision making based on local consultation, it is hard to see how the 2002 Act has boosted subsidiarity in practice. Had it done so, it may not have been necessary to change Auckland's governance.

## 5.5. The Auckland Experiment

### 5.5.1. The Royal Commission on Auckland Governance

Auckland has been governed by seven local (territorial) councils and one regional council since 1989. There has been a concern—fuelled by business interests since 1999—that the region is not doing well economically and that this reflects a failure of governance (Le Heron and McDermott, 2007). This led to the setting up of a Royal Commission to inquire into, investigate, and report on the local government arrangements (including institutions, mechanisms, and processes) that are required in the Auckland region over the foreseeable future in order to maximize, in a cost effective manner,

1. The current and future well-being of the region and its communities; and
2. The region's contribution to wider national objectives and outcomes (Le Heron and McDermott, 2007)

While the commissioners were required to "consult with the public in a way that allows people to express clearly their views on issues relating to local government arrangements for the Auckland region," no guidance was included as to the weight that might be given to submissions.

The Commission's conclusions were shaped by the view that economic performance had been compromised by poor coordination among councils and a failure to engage with communities and by the presumption that boosting economic performance depended on resolving governance problems. Its solution was much the same as previous reforms: restructure to increase capacity and save costs:

16. How local government is structured is important in determining what gets done—and what does not—in Auckland. Governance arrangements affect the capacity to plan and make strategic investments on an integrated, region-wide basis, and the ability to solve the larger and longer-term challenges effectively. Governance arrangements affect how much access people and communities have to the system and their ability to influence decisions about what services and initiatives they value. How local government is structured affects the cost of services and whether good value for money is delivered, the resources made available for investment, and service provision. (Royal Commission on Auckland Governance, 2009, p. 4)

The Royal Commission acknowledged the significance of community engagement, but simply echoed its treatment two decades earlier by reducing it to the capacity of citizens to participate. The discussion of local democracy was limited mainly to the efficiency of consultation and how community boards have—or have not—worked in the past.

20. Formal consultation by Auckland councils has become a poor proxy for true connection with their communities. Consultation and decision-making processes are prolonged and duplicative, and often fail to

provide a true measure of what citizens want, and what is in their best interests. These are not necessarily the same thing, and leadership is needed to draw people into well-informed debates about choices. The result of poor engagement is poor or delayed decision making, with elected leaders and officials finding it hard to do their jobs effectively. (Royal Commission on Auckland Governance, 2009, p. 4)

Interestingly, there is no mention of *subsidiarity* in the commission's eight-hundred-page report. This is consistent with an expectation that greater gains will arise from consolidating and centralizing functions, legitimating decisions through consultation, and delivering services through consolidated organizations rather than looking more closely at the capacity of communities or civil society.

Despite many submitters to the Royal Commission commenting on "the city's cultural diversity and its unique environment, history, and traditions including the identities of the city's constituent communities" (Royal Commission on Auckland Governance, 2009, p. 53), greater weight was given to the view that consolidating local government would strengthen the region's ability to deal with central government and to present a united front internationally.

### 5.5.2. Royal Commission Recommendations

The key recommendation from the Commission was for the replacement of the existing councils with a unitary council, recombining the tasks of policy development, regulation, and implementation, and internalizing environmental management, economic promotion, and community development. The new council would operate through two levels of "governance," a single elected council as the principal body, overseeing six elected "local councils." The Commission recommended that councilors should be elected both by wards and "at large," the latter to retain a region-wide perspective. However, central government decided that all councilors should be elected by geographic ward. While increasing the lip service paid to local democracy this also maintains divisions around traditional local communities of interest, albeit inside the new structure.

An executive mayor—a first in New Zealand—is elected at large and appoints an independent advisory staff. However, the mayoral office was created without the executive powers normally associated with a strong mayor. Control continues to reside in the council.

In deference to the Treaty of Waitangi, provision was made by the Commission for a quota of Māori representatives on the Auckland

Council drawn from local tribes.[2] However, the government replaced this with a Māori Advisory Board, whose members would have voting rights on some council committees.

Council Controlled Organizations are charged with region-wide delivery of infrastructure services, waterfront development, and economic promotion.

Much of the debate surrounding the establishment of a single city for Auckland was focused on tension between a council geared toward promoting economic development and one designed around the needs of communities. However, the main driver has been the quest for efficiency and reduced bureaucracy:

> No more costly duplications of functions across eight rating authorities, seven district plans and a multitude of differing bylaws. [ ... ] The focus will be on lowering fees and costs and simplifying the paper work under a single district plan. I can confidently say that ratepayers can now expect efficiency gains in the years ahead from integrated long-term planning and decision-making. (Minister's Speech, 3rd Reading, Local Government Auckland Law Reform Bill, June 6, 2010)

The impression is left that the reform has weakened local democracy and reduced subsidiarity at the local level, although, perhaps, strengthening the potential for the region as a whole to assume functions that have previously been held by central government. Even this seems unlikely, however, as central government effectively replaced the Royal Commission as the architect of the reforms, at the same time as it strengthened its own presence in Auckland.

The governance challenge—responding effectively to local needs through democratic processes—remains. It is likely to be made more difficult by the organizational model adopted for the new council. This has seen the resurrection of professional and functional divisions as an organizing principle within a new bureaucratic city structure, with the physical separation of those functions into offices distributed across the region. This in turn creates the problem of linking strong functional divisions with weak local agencies.

## 5.6. A COMPARISON

This section reflects on the reforms in local government that have taken place in New Zealand and Lombardy, although the comparison is clearly qualified by differences of scale and history. Lombard region has more people than New Zealand as a whole. Despite the centralist model in New Zealand—in practice if not in theory—services may still be defined and delivered closer to the people than those in Italy. This is simply because limited size creates a greater intimacy in politics—proximity between the governors and the governed—even with just two tiers of government.

Apart from obvious contextual differences, there are important differences in overall approach:

1. Subsidiarity is deeply embedded in the European discourse on governance at all levels, although there are clearly still concerns about the impersonal and remote nature of many government institutions. While community engagement has been important in New Zealand's reforms, the empowerment and responsiveness implicit in subsidiarity have not;
2. There is a strong focus on citizenship and its relationship with government at transnational, national, and regional level underlying the evolution of subsidiarity in Lombardy. The issue of local government is approached in a more instrumental manner in New Zealand;
3. Subsidiarity has informed reform in Lombardy. The new public economics and associated theories have played a greater part in New Zealand;
4. There is a direct and growing relationship between Lombardy's regional government and the institutions that make up civil society. Horizontal subsidiarity is weak in New Zealand unless considered in terms of the use of corporate agencies for the supply of services;
5. Civil society and voluntary society appear strong in Italy, and provide for diverse partnerships, contracts, and compacts with regional government. While volunteerism is traditionally strong in New Zealand its relationship with local government is limited;
6. In Lombardy, vouchers and user subsidies help create competition as part of a commitment to quasi markets. Local government in New Zealand does not act in this way, although it uses market-based procurement for services;
7. New Zealand operates a model of participation as democracy, fashioned around consultation and accountability. It is not clear from the material reviewed how far Lombardy goes down this path of engaging citizens at large through participation and consultation.

The prospect of increased diversity and capacity among the agencies of government is, in the case of Lombardy, driven by the imperative of ensuring the freedoms of citizens, families, and communities in the face of increasingly complex governance arrangements. In New

Zealand, the Auckland case suggests that the imperative continues to be defined primarily in economic terms.

While the Lombard model has demonstrated the practicality of subsidiarity-informed governance, it has some way to go. To the extent that it operates through quasi-market mechanisms—promoting nongovernmental providers and increasing citizen choice as drivers of capacity and competence—it resembles the efficiency-driven reforms that have been more to the fore in New Zealand.

### 5.6.1. Structuring Government around Subsidiarity

The differences can be illustrated by the links between different levels of government in the New Zealand and Lombardy (see Figure 5.1).

In the latter case all levels are relevant, with the relationship with the EU all-pervasive. The European Charter is based in part on a relationship between the EU and individual citizens. Hence, regional government has an intermediary role to play through its relationship with the EU, its association with other regions within and outside national borders, and the delegation of duties from central government. Given the significance of these roles and the potential to make a difference to regional and local outcomes, Lombardy pursues horizontal subsidiarity through its relationship with civil society.

New Zealand's central government crosses over the provincial/state/regional tier, with local government (districts, cities, regions, and unitary councils) subordinate to it. There is also less likelihood that horizontal subsidiarity can be easily adopted in New Zealand. Local government functions are limited. There is a whole realm of social activity—education, social support, social housing, and health—in which devolution, where it does take place, is between central government and local agents, such as school and district health boards.

Figure 5.1, given above, compares the different levels and structure of government agencies in New Zealand and Italy, and indicates the overlap and links among them.

### 5.7. Can New Zealand Offer Lessons for Lombardy?

The Lombard model highlights the vertical and horizontal relationships that build on—and build—the notion of citizenship at a transnational level while providing a framework for reconciling different levels of national and intranational government. The focus is on

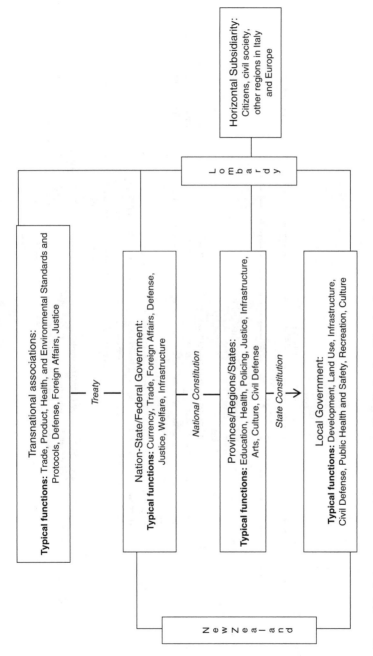

**Figure 5.1** Intergovernmental Arrangements, New Zealand and Lombardy

*Source:* The author's own chart, 2010.

**Table 5.1** Comparing Governance Arrangements, New Zealand and Lombardy

| | New Zealand | Italy |
|---|---|---|
| Transnational Arrangements | Primarily regional trade and defense agreements; British Commonwealth membership; close relationship with Australia. | European Union, NATO. |
| National Constitution | Parliamentary democracy, no written constitution; allocation of functions by central government; legislative house of representatives, executive cabinet of ministers, independent judiciary. | Constitutional democratic republic; legislative parliament with directly elected representatives, council of ministers and prime minister executive, independent judiciary. |
| Regional Government | Regional government is an arm of local government, with narrowly prescribed functions and no authority over local councils; funded by property taxes (rates), government grants (transport), and user charges. | Regions, presidential representative democracy based on councils, *giunta* (executive), and executive president. Limited executive competence; finance and resources mainly controlled by central government. Form of government subject to regional laws and statutes. |
| Local Government | Local councils are controlled by central statute although power of general competence means in theory they can range over a number of matters, subject to procedural compliance; funded by rates, government subsidies, user charges. | Provinces and towns are administrative divisions of regions; prefect represents central government plus elected representatives for council, *giunta*, and executive mayor/president. Many provinces grouped into consortia and towns into unions to deliver services. |

| | | |
|---|---|---|
| Citizen Participation | Heavy emphasis on consultative procedural compliance to validate policy—the emphasis in court has been on consultation having been done in good faith rather than on the substance of resulting decisions. | Subject to regional statute; state law protects right of participation for town or province, influenced by local practice. Through civil society, volunteerism, and capacity to exercise choice (supported in some sectors by the regional council). |
| Service Delivery | Limited reliance on civil society; increasing reliance on the market through applying managerial principles to single-purpose agencies for the quasi-commercial delivery of services, or through privatization of delivery by means of purchasing or contracting from private sector operators, or council-controlled organizations. | Local government meets basic service needs of the community—waste, water, sewer, street lighting, urban transportation—subject to separation between ownership and service, bidding processes. |
| Civil Society | Voluntarism is strong, but mainly independent of government. It may be facilitated by local government but engagement is limited. Importance of indigenous people. | Strong, traditional civil society, shaped in large part by church-based groups. |

*Source:* Author's own elaboration, 2010.

increasing the capacity of regional government to influence outcomes in the programs over which it has influence or authority.

Local government in New Zealand has been shaped by central government for 140 years—in a nation that is only 170 years old. The notion of subsidiarity does not feature strongly. Any discourse touching on decentralization has focused heavily on representation (e.g., Forgie et al., 1999). By comparison with Lombardy, local government in New Zealand can be seen as a compromise between efficiency and democracy based on managerial principles. Democracy depends heavily on electoral representation overlain by a commitment to consultation.

Despite these differences and the minor role played by subsidiarity, the New Zealand experience of the past two decades with its emphasis on efficiency and accountability suggests some questions that can be directed at Lombardy's governance model.

1. What is the role of local councils?

Although based on only limited material, the review here suggests that Lombardy may be able to progress through further vertical subsidiarity by engagement with local government: provinces, towns, and their subregional associations. Local governments may act as "agents" of regional government through vertical subsidiarity and may also introduce further opportunities for horizontal subsidiarity through their own associations with local civil society.

2. Do you need a regional tier between central and local government? Going further, would there be any gains in reducing the role of regional government and merging some of the smaller local councils, increasing their capacity to deal either more directly with the center or more effectively with the regional government?

The likelihood is that even if a gain in the effectiveness of local government is possible from such a change, history, culture, and scale are against it. It may be better for regions to explore options to boost subsidiarity by delegating functions to provinces and towns, although this might require consolidation of very small units.

More generally, multiple tiers of government increase opportunities for locating functions at the most appropriate level—central, regional, local, or even village. This may call for protocols, mentoring, guidelines, or joint ventures to increase cooperation both between regional and local government and among small units to create the capacity to meet needs at the lowest levels.

An increased emphasis on localism might simply mean looking to local government to identify more opportunities to pursue horizontal subsidiarity rather than diminishing the region's role.

### 3. Is it possible to enforce subsidiarity?

In New Zealand there is a strong statutory commitment to consultation. Within Auckland, there was a history of collaboration across councils before the 2010 amalgamation (McDermott, 2009). As it stands, local authorities are required by the Local Government Act to prepare an agreement every three years on how they intend to collaborate. This raises the question of whether it was necessary for Auckland's councils to merge rather than require them to pursue more effective community engagement by way of horizontal subsidiarity.

Despite a history of collaboration and consultation, there has been little investigation of the most appropriate level of government for any given role or the most appropriate roles for different levels of government. Could subsidiarity be encouraged by regulation?

It is not clear whether a degree of compulsion might accelerate progress in Lombardy. Ultimately subsidiarity implies voluntary or associative assignment of roles, which becomes most likely if funding moves with them, and if the capacity exists at different levels of government.

Perhaps the better approach in both countries is to facilitate subsidiarity by fostering a supportive rather than coercive environment underpinned by developing the capacity of civil society, and to fund it to act when the competence exists.

### 4. How are electoral representation and subsidiarity related?

The range of candidates and voter turnout at elections reveal citizen engagement with *representative* local government. If greater engagement is associated with strong subsidiarity, electoral representation and choice of candidates should increase with adoption of the principles of subsidiarity.

On these grounds, representative democracy may be strengthened by subsidiarity-based governance. Conversely, subsidiarity-based governance will be enhanced by strong electoral outcomes that give greater legitimacy to any delegations put in place. These are not alternative so much as complementary forms of democracy. Boosting both is presumably necessary for stronger local democracy. Greater subsidiarity may well lead to more meaningful elections.

5. What is the role of consultation in subsidiarity?

In New Zealand there is a legal requirement for councils to consult and to be open minded about the information they receive, but there is no compulsion to act on it. Responsibility and accountability remain focused on process more than the quality of decisions and outcomes.

Consultation does not guarantee that functions will be assigned to the most appropriate level of government or to the most effective agency. Nor does it guarantee that policy programs will address all the expectations of the citizenry. It does give the public a voice, though, and the *potential* to influence where and how functions might be delivered. Under a subsidiarity-based model, this should increase the legitimacy of delegations.

6. Should citizens be more involved in policy formation?

Equally, the practice of subsidiarity does not guarantee a meaningful or balanced citizen input into policy or program design. However, policy and program evaluation should address how far citizen engagement lifts the quality of decisions and outcomes associated with increasing subsidiarity.

In Lombardy it may not be enough merely to draw on civil society and its particular competencies for enhancing service delivery. The prioritizing of services and spending and the quality of services delivered should benefit from the strong, parallel engagement of citizens in policy development. This may best be developed at the regional level, to ensure that the implementation of policy through subsidiarity is well founded and well directed in terms of actual community needs and preferences. Involving citizens in decision making at the regional level should improve both policy development and subsequent checks and balances on implementation.

7. How involved are the communities?

However, excessive consultation can paradoxically lead to a sense of disempowerment because the process becomes trivialized. It is important that councils strike a sound balance between the significance of the matter at hand, the intensity of engagement, and its capacity to respond to the results.

The increasingly diverse nature of communities raises other issues. It is important that in reaching decisions care is taken to seek the views of groups that might not be involved for reasons like inaccessibility, difficult communications, apathy, ignorance, or disenchantment.

8. Can a market model strengthen subsidiarity?

The New Zealand model favors commercial or quasi-commercial arrangements for service definition and delivery. Many councils contract out development and maintenance of infrastructure. Some activities have been placed in council-controlled organizations, directed by appointed boards recruited from the private sector. They are required to operate in a commercial manner. Very little, however, has been assigned, delegated, or contracted to nonprofit bodies.

The question is whether assigning some services to a market model enhances local government's capacity to deliver on others? The shift from community to market-driven service definition and delivery is a subtle one. On occasion, the latter may usefully play into the hands of the former by better enabling governments to concentrate on providing public goods and meeting public needs and reducing their focus on services that can be effectively delivered through the market.

9. How to keep the civil in civil society?

The reluctance of local councils to delegate in New Zealand may reflect concerns over the capacity of civil society to deliver and over accountability for service failures. The specialist skills required for fulfilling particular responsibilities, maintaining standards, complying with delivery requirements, and monitoring outcomes become scarcer closer to the ground.

Experience with community management of recreational facilities in Auckland, for example, revealed several constraints (CityScope Consultants 2005; Dunbar, 2006):

1. The limited size and ageing of the voluntary sector and its members, particularly in socially deprived areas;
2. The growing list of health, safety, security, and accounting compliance requirements coupled with scarce management and accounting skills in the voluntary sector;
3. Consequently, the potential for either abuse of the system or mistakes, which undermine the trust or confidence necessary to encourage functional delegation or transfer.

Where there are small numbers, or scarce resources and skills, unrepresentative individuals or groups may exert control over community resources and facilities for their own ends. Alternatively, the result may be service and control failures and a need for the center to reassert its control.

Subsidiarity requires a high level of competence and transparency within civil society, and trust between the regional or local council and nongovernmental agents. It calls for continuous capacity building—training, mentoring, institutional development, and financial support—and monitoring.

## 5.8. CONCLUSION: BOOSTING THE CAPACITY OF CIVIL SOCIETY

The experience of local governance varies between New Zealand and Lombardy, although both seek more effective and efficient local government. In the former case, giving citizens an opportunity to be heard through consultation is the basis for building participation, although it may not promote subsidiarity. In Lombardy, increasing the community presence and responsibility for decision making and implementation is the favored model. One of the issues raised in this chapter is the legitimizing of the policies and programs that might be delegated through subsidiarity and especially how far legitimacy is conferred by citizen engagement in policy formation.

The New Zealand experience draws attention to the role that different methods of consultation might play in ensuring that programs for local delivery also reflect local input at the policy design stage.

In both cases a key to extending subsidiarity is building capacity within civil society. There are challenges, including demands on people's time and resources, and the technical requirements for compliance, which do not necessarily come with volunteerism.

Boosting civil society might also be addressed by making it easier for institutions to get involved. This may be to do with tax treatment, with material rewards, and through encouraging nonprofit organizations to collaborate where resources are thin. In Lombardy there may also be merit in exploring the capacity of local councils to play a more active role.

Finally, it can be argued that market models may have played too great a role in reshaping New Zealand local government, reducing local democracy. Offsetting this, though, is the prospect that well-directed market delivery of some services will enable councils to concentrate on core areas of community development. The possibility that a subsidiarity-based model of devolution and delegation will assume the character of neoliberal reform is most likely to be avoided if managerial or quasi-market models are used to enhance the ability of local government to meet core public needs through working effectively with civil society.

## NOTES

1. McDermott and Forgie (1999) did demonstrate that while physical infrastructure continued to dominate council spending during the 1990s, New Zealand "local government is in the process of realigning its mandate, increasing its focus on the well-being of people as it reduces its spending on services to property" (p. 259).
2. This is consistent with the seven seats reserved for voting by Māori constituents only in New Zealand's current Parliament. The number varies according to the number of people registered on the Māori Electoral Roll.

## REFERENCES

CityScope Consultants (2005) *Community Needs Assessment* (Auckland: Report to Auckland City Council).Colombo, A. (2008) "The 'Lombardy model': Subsidiarity-informed regional governance" in *Social Policy and Administration*, 42(2), 177–96.

Colombo, A., and T. O'Sullivan (2012) "The Lombardy region, economic and institutional features, an experience in government" in (ed. with A. Brugnoli) *Government, Governance and Welfare Reform. Structural Changes and Subsidiarity in Italy and Britain* (Cheltenham: E-Elgar) [forthcoming].

Constitutional Arrangements Committee (2005) *Inquiry to Review New Zealand's Existing Constitutional Arrangements* (Wellington: House of Representatives).

Controller and Auditor General (2010) *Matters Arising from the 2009–19 Long-Term Council Community Plans* (Wellington: Parliamentary Paper, Office of the Auditor).

Department of Internal Affairs (2009) *Observations and Trends From 2009/19 Long-Term Council Community Plans* (Wellington: Local Government Information Series 15).

Dunbar, R. (2006) "Development models for diverse communities: Subsidiarity, partnerships and accountability." Paper to the Congress of the New Zealand Planning Institute and the Planning Institute of Australia (Queensland).

Easton, B. (1997) *The Commercialisation of the State* (Auckland: Auckland University Press).

Elwood, B. (1995) "From theory to practice; The New Zealand experience" in P. McDermott, V. Forgie, and R. Howell (eds.), (1995) *An Agenda for Local Government, Proceeding of the New Local Government Conferences* (Palmerston North: Massey University), 309–16.

Forgie, V., C. Cheyne, and P. McDermott (1999) *Democracy in New Zealand Local Government: Purpose and Practice.* Occasional Paper 2 (Palmerston North: School of Resource and Environmental Planning, Massey University).

Giddens, A. (1998) *The Third Way: The Renewal of Social Democracy* (Cambridge: Polity Press).

Guerin, K. (2002) *Subsidiarity: Implications for New Zealand* (Wellington: New Zealand Treasury Working Paper 02/03).

Hamilton, A. (1788) *The Federalist Papers* (New York: J and A McLean).

Hewison, G. (2009) *a Critical Review of the Local Government Act 2002: Is It Working and Are Changes Necessary* (Auckland: Kensington Swan) (Accessed at www.kensingtonswan.com/Publications/Local%20 Authorities/Local_Government_Act_is_it_working.pdf).

Hirst, P., and V. Bader (2001) *Associative Democracy: The Real Third Way* (Oregon: Frank Cass & Co).

Hodgson, J. (2006) *Economics in the Shadows of Darwin and Marx: Essays on Institutional and Evolutionary Themes* (Cheltenham: Edward Elgar).

Howell, R., P. McDermott, and V. Forgie (1996) *The Unfinished Reform in Local Government: The Legacy and the Prospect.* Occasional Papers in Local Government Studies 3 (Palmerston North: Massey University).

IReR (2009) "Subsidiarity: Brief anthology" (Unpublished draft) Regione Lombardia.

Kawharau, I. H. (ed.) (1989) *Waitangi: Māori and Pakeha Perspectives of the Treaty of Waitangi* (Auckland: Oxford University Press).

Kelsey, J. (1995) *The New Zealand Experiment* (Auckland: Auckland University Press).

Le Heron, R., and P. McDermott (2007) "Auckland's metro project: A metropolitan governance strategy for regional economic development?" in C. Tamasy and M. Taylor, (eds.), *Globalising Worlds: Geographical Perspectives on New Economic Configurations* (Aldershot: Ashgate).

Lippi, A., and M. Morisi (2005) *Scienza dell'amministrazione* (Bologna: Il Mulino).

McDermott, P. (1995) "Recipes for reform. An agenda for local government in the new millennium" in P. McDermott, V. Forgie, and R. Howell (eds.), (1995) *An Agenda for Local Government, Proceeding of the New Local Government Conferences* (Palmerston North: Massey University), 1–20.

McDermott, P. (2009) *The Call for Integrated Planning. Report of the Royal Commission on Auckland Governance* (Auckland) (Vol. 4), 357–85.

McDermott, P., and V. Forgie (1999) "Trends in local government: Efficiency, functions and democracy" in *Political Science*, 50(2), 247–65.

Officials Coordinating Committee on Local Government (1988) *The Reform of Local and Regional Government* (Wellington: Department of Internal Affairs).

Palmer, G. (1995) "Local government, the constitution, and the future" in P. McDermott, V. Forgie, and R. Howell (eds.), (1995) *An Agenda for Local Government, Proceeding of the New Local Government Conferences* (Palmerston North: Massey University), 317–24.

Palmer, G., and M. Palmer (2004) *Bridled Power: New Zealand's Constitution and Government* (4th edition) (Melbourne: Oxford University Press).

Proudhon, P. (2000) *Del principio federativo* (Milano: Asefi) cited in IReR, 2009, 34–37.Reid, M. (1999) "The central-local government relationship" in *Political Science*, 50(2), 164–81.

Reid, M. (2001) "Local government reform—its here but what does it mean?" *Public Sector*,.24(2), 11–14

Royal Commission on Auckland Governance (2009) *Volume 1 Report* (Wellington, Department of Internal Affairs).

Royal Commission on Social Policy (1988) *The April Report: Report of the Royal Commission on Social Policy* (Wellington: The Commission).

Shand, D., G. Horsley, and C. Cheyne (2007) *Funding Local Government. Report of the Local Government Rates Inquiry* (Wellington, Department of Internal Affairs).

# Part II

# POLICY SECTORS

# 6

# Subsidiarity and Education in Lombardy: Limits and Possibilities

## Charles L. Glenn

## 6.1. Introduction

I thought that I knew something about the educational system in Italy, and especially in Lombardy, but this closer look has been for me full of surprises!

What I have discovered is a regional government that has been directing its social and economic policies on the basis of well-thought-out *ideas*, not simply responding to problems and opportunities. Perhaps that is the case elsewhere, but in my impression from comparative study of about fifty countries, the national and regional governments today tend to devote their efforts to adapting and adjusting their policies in an effort to remain faithful to the ideas that guided the formation of those policies in the 1950s and 1960s, rather than engaging in fundamental rethinking of their guiding principles.

What are those ideas? The French call it *l'État-providence*, the state that provides for its citizens, who by implication are unable to provide for themselves. In education, it is the idea that the state is uniquely able to create citizens through its own schools, subjecting them to a *pédagogie d'État* designed to mold their hearts and minds in a pattern approved by "experts" who know much better than parents what is in the interest of children.

Lombardy is apparently different. The regional government seems to be taking with great seriousness the implications of the principle of subsidiarity, and is prepared to experiment to try out how this principle can function in practice.

That might not seem so unusual; after all, the principle of subsidiarity was explicitly enshrined in the Treaty of Maastricht, and in theory it applies throughout the European Union. Three years ago I was invited, by Giorgio Vittadini, to respond to the Report *Sussidiarietà ed Educazione,* and quoted Vittadini's finding, on the part of many respondents, "il desiderio di essere tutelati e supportati dallo Stato."[1] In that context of public opinion, it is all the more striking that a government dependent upon popular support would systematically enact policies that require citizens to take more responsibility for themselves and their families, with the government in a supporting role, and to do so in the name of the principle of subsidiarity.

My report is organized in four parts. The first explores this concept of "subsidiarity" in a broader context of contemporary thinking about the role of civil society in assuming roles that had been taken over by governments in recent decades.

The second considers education in Lombardy in the context of national policies, and the severe limitations on the role of the regional government.

The third section describes how Lombardy has responded to these restrictions, and has employed its limited leverage in ways consistent with the principle of subsidiarity.

Finally, the fourth makes three proposals for how the region could play a more dynamic role in improving the quality of general education in Lombardy. One of these proposals would require action at the national level; the other two could perhaps be implemented by regional initiative alone.

## 6.2. Understanding Subsidiarity in the Lombard Model

Lombardy Regional Government documents mention "subsidiarity" often, and regional law specifies:

> La Regione, in attuazione del principio di sussidiarietà orizzontale, riconosce e favorisce l'autonoma iniziativa dei cittadini, singoli e associati, delle famiglie, delle formazioni e delle istituzioni sociali, delle associazioni e degli enti civili e religiosi, garantendo il loro apporto nella programmazione e nella realizzazione dei diversi interventi e servizi pubblici.[2]

Similarly, a recent regional government report comments:

> Viene così espresso un netto favore nei confronti di una cittadinanza di tipo attivo, in cui i cittadini, come singoli o associati, promuovono autonomamente iniziative di interesse generale: iniziative che poi la Regione, sulla base della normativa statutaria, è tenuta a riconoscere, sostenere e, soprattutto, integrare nelle proprie politiche.[3]

This emphasis seems to reflect—or to have created—a broad consensus, at least among leading elements in the region, about its significance for the progress that Lombardy has unquestionably experienced.

The principle of subsidiarity is in part a response to concern that government will overstep the limits of its appropriate role and begin to have an inappropriate influence upon its citizens, seeking to shape hearts and minds in a way that could lend itself to totalitarian agendas, a concern most strongly felt with respect to education. Popular schooling is the instrument that an activist government is most tempted to employ to bring about social transformation and that, having started to use, it is most likely to use evermore deliberately and extensively.

We now have many decades of experience with different arrangements for popular schooling, varying considerably among countries with generally similar political and social conditions. The experience with educational subsidiarity in Lombardy, partial as it is, offers a splendid opportunity to see how school autonomy and parental choice actually function in practice.

There are good reasons for government to continue an active role—perhaps even more active, in some respects, than at present—in ensuring that educational services are adequate and accessible, even as it turns to civil society institutions to deliver those services.

Subsidiarity in education is concerned not only with organizational forms and dynamics but also and more centrally with the spirit and the values that may animate schools and other institutions providing the human care of human beings. What they do and how they treat those entrusted to them is, for good or ill, the expression of deeply held beliefs about human life.

The right of parents to have access, for their children, to schooling with a distinctive character reflecting their own convictions and other than that provided by the state was established in international law after the World War II in response to the use of schooling by fascist regimes. The International Covenant on Economic, Social and Cultural Rights, adopted by the United Nations in 1966, was intended to set an international legal standard.

Article 13 is specific about the rights of parents and the rights of those who establish nongovernment schools.

> 3. The States Parties to the present Covenant undertake to have respect for the liberty of parents and, when applicable, legal guardians to choose for their children schools, other than those established by the public authorities, which conform to such minimum educational standards as may be laid down or approved by the State and to ensure the religious and moral education of their children in conformity with their own convictions.
>
> 4. No part of this article shall be construed so as to interfere with the liberty of individuals and bodies to establish and direct educational institutions, subject always to the observance of the principles set forth in paragraph I of this article and to the requirement that the education given in such institutions shall conform to such minimum standards as may be laid down by the State. (OHCHR website)

Unresolved was the question whether this language about educational freedom was intended simply to restrain the state from infringing upon the rights of parents, or whether it imposed an obligation upon the state to make it possible for parents to choose schools providing "religious and moral" education consistent with their own convictions. If only the former, it is obvious that many parents would not be in a position, for financial and other practical reasons, to act upon their choices.

The Committee on Economic, Social and Cultural Rights of the United Nations addressed this issue in 1999, in a "General Comment" on the right to education as spelled out in the Covenant on Economic, Social and Cultural Rights, including a significant set of four characteristics that an educational system should possess, one of which was as follows:

> Acceptability—the form and substance of education, including curricula and teaching methods, have to be acceptable (e.g. relevant, culturally appropriate and of good quality) to students and, in appropriate cases, parents. (UNHCHR website)

This criterion of "acceptability" gives a sort of Copernican twist to the process of determining whether a particular country is meeting its obligation to ensure that its citizens enjoy their right to education: only the pupil and his or her parents can decide whether the schooling provided is acceptable.

As in the principles that govern Lombardy, this criterion places the person—the user rather than the provider of education—at the center. Unfortunately, national law in Italy is largely unfriendly to this perspective, and does not ensure that all parents can exercise the fundamental right to select an acceptable school for their children.

### 6.2.1. Civil Society (Non-State) Schools in Italy

The emphasis, in public policy, upon defining common rules and then allowing autonomous application of these rules at the school level creates at least the possibility of "recognizing that the public character of a service does not depend upon its type of governance, but upon its adhesion to common rules." The state, on this model, would become the guarantor and promoter of education rather than, as now, its nearly monopolistic provider (the proportion of pupils in nonstate schools in Italy, though it is growing steadily, is well below the EU average). Perhaps, some hope, the stress upon autonomy represents an important stage in the evolution from a school intended as an ideological apparatus of the State and as a bureaucratic structure governed centrally from on high, to one which expresses the communities which make up civil society. (Malizia and Stenco, 1999, p. 50)

Consistent with this new emphasis, the law on norms for "equivalent" schools, adopted in March 2000, defines them, in part, as schools that respond to the educational demands of families, as well as to various quality requirements. "Equivalence [*parità*] is recognized in the case of independent schools which request it and which [ ... ] commit themselves expressly" to comply with various requirements. Thus, it is not left up to the discretion of government officials whether or not to provide this recognition.

The law claims to offer "entire freedom with respect to cultural orientation and pedagogical/didactic approach." In carefully balanced yet finally ambiguous language, the law specifies that "taking account of the educational project of the school, the instruction is marked by the principles of liberty established in the Constitution." Does this mean that the distinctive character of a school can place a limit on how it expresses these "principles of liberty," or that the latter place a limit on the possibilities for a school's distinctive character? Obviously, the second interpretation could be used to limit severely the freedom of a school to express an understanding of culture and human nature distinctively different from that prevailing in society.

It should be noted that, at least at present, the acquisition of this status does not create an entitlement to public subsidy. Independent schools in most regions of Italy receive no public subsidy. Italy is unusual compared with most other members of the European Union in this respect.

Critics like Mario Mauro charge that teacher union officials and bureaucrats who block funding for pupils attending independent schools are "living from consolidated privileges" and are afraid to see the quality of the services they provided judged by the choices of free citizens rather than by the norms that they themselves have established. "Social racism consists in maintaining the state monopoly [of free schooling] so that the rich can use the schools that they wish, state or non-state," while those who are not rich are limited to what is provided for their children by the state system, or to seeking a charitable alternative. "Parity is not charity [*parità non è carità*]!" (Mauro, 1999, pp. 22–23).

Although there is no general, nationwide funding for independent schools, several regional governments have made moves in this direction. The regional law 14/91 in Friuli Venezia Giulia, for example, extended support to families whose children attended "obligatory and secondary schools [which are] non-state, authorized, equivalent, legally recognized," on the grounds that equal treatment of pupils in state and nonstate schools was guaranteed by the constitution. The province took further measures in 2000:

> In the context of actions intended to support the exercise of the right to schooling [ ... ] the Region implements initiatives to ensure conditions of equality [*parità*] of citizens in access to the various levels and types of schools, showing respect for the autonomous educational choices of the family. (Regione Friuli Venezia Giulia, Regional Law no. 9, article 1.1.)

Similarly, Emilia Romagna stated, in 1999, that the region and local governments would favor the creation of an "integrated educational system for the right to instruction, based upon an increasing coordination and cooperation among the various providers of education, while respecting autonomy and pedagogical-didactic identity, freedom of teaching, and also the freedom of families to make educational choices."

Piedmont, Veneto, and other regions have made provisions for funding part of the cost of pupils attending nonstate schools, under arrangements designated as "scholarships" (*borse di studio*), "reimbursement of costs" (*rimborso spese*), or "school vouchers" (*buoni scuola*), and typically limited to families with below-average incomes.

Lombardy has taken the most extensive action, as we will see in the third section.

Recent emphasis, in Italian policy discussion, on promoting the autonomy of individual public schools would appear to remove one of the major barriers to recognizing the position and contributions of independent schools. After all, if a single model of school is no longer regarded as essential in the interest of national unity and of justice, the rationale for suspicion of independent schools largely falls away. Certainly this is the case in Lombardy, with its commitment to the principle of subsidiarity, though at the national level the emphasis on school autonomy seems largely rhetorical.

## 6.3. LIMITATIONS ON REGIONAL AUTHORITY IN EDUCATION IN LOMBARDY

Regional governments in Italy do not at present have authority over schools providing general instruction, despite the provisions of the Bassanini Law and Section V of the constitution as amended in 2001. Their major scope for influencing general education is through nonstate or independent schools, and it is in this respect that Lombardy has shown itself most creative in its implementation of policies on the basis of subsidiarity.

The Italian educational system has been strongly centralized since the unification of Italy in the nineteenth century. The state–controlled school was seen as the instrument of choice for making one nation and teaching a standard form of Italian to all of its children. Successive Italian governments created a monopolistic, centralized, and bureaucratic educational system.

In many cases, however, it was only through private—often religious—initiatives that schooling were provided, and the government was forced to abandon any intentions that it may have had to secularize schools and instruction. Because of the government's lack of resources and executive effectiveness, the Catholic Church and its teaching orders continued to provide a large proportion of the schooling available.

Despite the ineffective implementation of the Casati Law (1859, 1861), its goals and underlying assumptions were consistent with what we could call the program of the enlightened bourgeoisie and intellectuals in other contemporary European societies. These included an intended primacy of state schooling over religious schools, with a program of popular enlightenment intended to lead to social pacification, national loyalty, and economic modernization, not to real social change.

One of the priorities of the fascist regime, accomplished in 1923, was to adopt legislation subjecting the entire educational system to closer control by the state. In 1923 the journal *Critica Fascista* wrote that

> the school is the strongest weapon by which a State such as the Italian State can maintain and guarantee the spiritual unity of the Nation. This is not a function which can be entrusted to private industry, but is the highest expression of the State understood as a moral activity. (Charnitzky, 1996, pp. 149–50, 182)

In 1925, the Rector of the Catholic University of the Sacred Heart in Milan wrote of "the battle for the freedom of schools," threatened both by the claim of the state to an exclusive right to operate schools and also by administrative interference with the operation of schools, and he added that the liberal doctrine also denies real freedom in that it denies both the absolute right of parents to educate their children and the right of the church to exercise its divine teaching authority. The implicit conflict with the fascist state became even clearer with the publication of the encyclical on education, *Divini Illius Magistri*, significantly published first in Italian.

Obviously, the debate over subsidiarity in Italian education goes back a long way. Both the liberal and the fascist governments that ruled united Italy identified civil society and the state, and the post-war governments have inherited this tendency to see education as an "ideological apparatus of the State" rather than as an expression of an independent civil society.

The continued strength of the model of educational uniformity in Italian political circles has been attributed to "a disease of ideologizing at all costs," leading to policies that are "protectionist, anachronistic, and hostile to improvements" (Ribolzi, 2000, p. 7). Not that government actually has much power to promote reforms in schools; "the Italian system associates the maximum of formalism with the minimum of real control" (Ribolzi, 1987, p. 81). Or, as another author put it:

> The prevailing model of school in Italy, statist and centralizing, does not work anymore, is no longer able to ensure an adequate service. At this point the problem of freedom of schools is not only a question of principle, of a value in which one might believe or not. It has

become a question of confronting in operational terms whether one wants to ensure an efficient educational service for the country. (Valli, 1991, p. 4)

Despite recent gestures in the direction of decentralization of decision making to regional and local authorities, and to schools, the educational system remains a single organization with 12,000 principals, more than 700,000 teachers, 150,000 other staff, and 7 million pupils in 13,000 schools. Compared with the European Union average, the proportion of pupils in state schools (93 percent) is high. Per-pupil costs are also high in Italy, well above the EU average; these high costs are attributable in large part to the unusually large number of teachers in relation to the number of pupils, especially as enrolments have fallen in recent years with demographic decline.

While the Bassanini Law (1997) called for implementing legislation to decentralize some administrative functions and tasks to the regions and local authorities, including responsibility for schools, this has not occurred.

In recent years, Italian policy has moved toward a greater recognition of the advantages of school autonomy, but the habits of bureaucratic centralization have proved resistant. Article 21 of regional law 59/1997 established the legal personality of individual schools, but without conferring upon them effective authority to shape their own distinctive programs or to control their staffing and budgets.

A national regulation issued in 1999 and effective September 2000 defined the purposes of school autonomy in the state sector as follows:

> The autonomy of schools is a guarantee of educational freedom and of cultural pluralism and supports the planning and realization of educational efforts aimed at the development of human persons, responsive to various contexts, to the demands of families, and to the specific characteristics of the persons involved, in order to guarantee them educational success, consistent with the goals and objectives of the educational system and with the necessity of improving the effectiveness of the process of education and learning. (Presidenza della Repubblica, 1999, article 1.2)

The regulations require each school to develop an educational plan (*piano dell'offerta formativa*). This plan is to be developed with broad participation, and is to serve as the "fundamental constitutive document" of the cultural and programmatic identity of the school and to make explicit the curricular, extracurricular, educational, and organizational arrangements that the individual school is adopting within the scope of its autonomy. It must be consistent with the general and educational objectives of the different types of schooling promulgated nationally and must also reflect the demands of the local cultural, social, and economic realities as well as regional planning for educational provision. The latter must take into account different methodological options, including those of minority groups, and give weight to professional expertise.

Schools are granted a certain latitude in shaping their instruction through this planning process, taking into account the instructional freedom of teachers, the freedom of educational choice on the part of families, and the general goals of the educational system. They may, for example, adapt the time devoted to the various subjects in order to respond to the instructional emphasis of the school and the "rhythm of learning" of the pupils, or put together multiage groupings or combine several subjects in an interdisciplinary way. Several informants have suggested to me, however, that school directors seldom make effective use of this margin of discretion, since little in their training or previous experience prepares them to be creative leaders. This is one of the issues that would have to be addressed in Lombardy for real subsidiarity to flourish in general education: policy changes are not enough without parallel changes in mentality, and little in the training and experience of most educators prepares them to be entrepreneurial in a positive sense.

A school may adopt any organizational model that expresses its freedom to plan and which is consistent with the general and specific goals of the type of education that it provides, as a means of promoting and sustaining the innovation process and the improvement of its educational offerings. Teacher assignments may be modified in response to the methodological and organizational choices made in the school's educational plan.

These measures in the direction of autonomy are placed firmly within a context of national definition of curriculum goals, timetables, and specific learning objectives so that the unitary character of the national educational system is protected (*è garantito il carattere unitario del sistema di istruzione*). The curriculum laid down nationally may be supplemented with elective courses, in consultation with regional and local officials.

As a result of this continuing legal monopoly by the national government of the provision of general education, the role of the region of Lombardy has been limited to influencing schools "from the outside." It has done so imaginatively and in ways that offer promise for future developments, but not at present with a reach that permits the fundamental reforms needed by Italian education.

It seems clear, however, that the region is prepared to go farther. In the latest report of the Directorate General of Education, Training and Labour, the final section, entitled "Contributi per la nona legislatura,"[4] the discussion of *innovatività* notes the need to "ridefinire ruoli e funzioni in sintonia con un contesto legislativo nazionale in profondo cambiamento, che vede concretizzarsi quelle maggiori responsabilità a livello regionale che la Lombardia da tempo anticipa ed è pronto ad assumere."[5] More specifically, it calls for legislative action at the national and regional level, in words that I would endorse fully as essential for the reforms that general education in the region requires:

> Il processo in atto, che vede la Regione come attore chiave delle politiche di istruzione e formazione, in attuazione della riforma del Titolo V delle Costituzione, troverà nuovo impulso dalla piena attuazione del federalismo fiscale. Tale linea di sviluppo vede la sua piena realizzazione nella IX legislatura, che raccoglierà i risultati del autonomia e della responsabilizzazione delle scuole, liberate dall'attuale gestione centralistica e burocratica che ne limita le capacità propositive e di innovazione. L'esito di questo processo si raggiungerà alla piena autonomia significa innanzitutto affidare agli istituti la propria gestione economica, la selezione diretta e la titolarità del rapporto di lavoro del personale, in direzione di una più efficace amministrazione delle risorse e di una valorizzazione degli insignanti, attraverso il riconoscimento, anche economico, della carriera e del merito. Autonomia e responsabilizzazione delle scuole non comportano una riduzione della responsabilità regionale. La Regione è un attore importante non solo per garantire la sostenibilità economica e finanziaria ma anche per le funzioni di controllo e programmazione.[6]
>
> (Regione Lombardia Direzione Generale Istruzione, Formazione e Lavoro, 2010, p. 188 and p. 191)

My recommendations in section four of this report are fully consistent with this position.

### 6.3.1. Integration of Immigrants and their Children

The most damaging aspect of the limited authority of the region over general education, in my view, is that its policymakers lack what should be their most effective instrument for addressing the integration of the residents of foreign origin (including those born in Lombardy of foreign-born parents) who constitute a significant proportion of the population. Some 10 percent of the pupils in the lower levels of schooling in Lombardy are of foreign origin, and this proportion is growing rapidly; it grew from only 2 percent in 1998–1999. At the end of 2008 there were more than 900,000 foreigners living in Lombardy, about 23 percent of the total for Italy, and more than half a million are from outside the EU.

The fact that this aspect of the social dynamic of Lombardy was not mentioned by any of those whom I interviewed, unless I brought it up, and is discussed only in passing in the many documents I have reviewed, must surely, in part, reflect the absence of the region from the daily operations of general education, where the presence of immigrants, in any society, is most directly experienced, and where the most important interventions occur, or do not. It is true that the report of the Direzione Generale Istruzione, Formazione e Lavoro states, as one of its goals,

> sostenere l'unità tra le fasce della popolazione, i diversi territori, le diverse articolazioni economiche e culturali, valorizzando le differenze e le peculiarità di ogni realtà, poiché coesione non significa omologazione ma moltiplicazione delle opportunità per tutti.[7]
>
> (Regione Lombardia Direzione Generale Istruzione, Formazione e Lavoro, 2010, p. 189)

At several points in the same report, it is evident that the programs implemented by the region for those who have not completed the normally required level of education are serving youth and adults from outside the EU; this is especially the case with the program for "Dispersione Scolastica." Such pupils are also eligible for the "Dote Scuola per l'Istruzione" (see next section), of course, but no information is provided about the extent to which that is leading to successful programs of integration into Italian society at a critical age for acquisition of both language and culture.

I should add that I raised this issue with Director General Giuseppe Colosio of the *Ufficio Scolastico Regionale*—representative of the national ministry and thus responsible for general education in Lombardy—and it was clear that he shares this concern and is making efforts to address it, within the limited policy instruments at his disposal. His responses to my questions in general were those of a concerned educator and not the routine self-justification of a bureaucrat, and he was honest about the difficulties of influencing the system in a positive direction.

It is crucial that Lombardy implement effective policies for the integration of the younger generation of immigrants into the norms of Italian society, and the skills that society requires. A number of Italian sociologists of education have taken up this theme, and it is evident that there is a growing risk of alienation of immigrant youth, parallel to what has been seen with unfortunate and not-yet-resolved results in France, England, and the Netherlands. How to address the issue without exacerbating anti-immigrant sentiments among the general population is a matter of great delicacy, but doing so should not be postponed.

### 6.3.2. The Exception: Vocational Training

Although the region has limited authority over general education, it has since the State-Regional Conference of February 2009—full responsibility for vocational training (*formazione professionale*), and its efforts in this area provide an excellent example of what it *could* be doing in general education as well, if it possessed the authority and the resources to do so.

In discussion with two leaders in this field, I was told that in recent years there had been a transformation of thinking about *formazione professionale* from providing a two-year program to get youth off the streets and provide them with some basic skills for work, seen as a necessity rather than as a calling, to offering a three-or-more year program with inclusion of academic subjects. In this way, youth are prepared more adequately for adulthood in Italian society, and the idea of work itself is given increased dignity. In turn, in the words of the Direzione Generale Istruzione, Formazione e Lavoro, this has led to a recognition of the equal dignity of vocational education, with the addition of a fourth year leading to a diploma, and a fifth year leading to the national examination for admission to university.

Lombardy is, thus, offering a model for other regions of the development—though there is still much to do—of a dual system of education with equivalent respect shown for the two alternatives. The fact that some youth are going on from *formazione professionale* to university, while commendable, should not detract from the significance of a thorough vocational education as an end in itself. My only question is how this relates to the secondary technical education that is still under the control of the national government. Vocational and technical education should form a single continuum.

An important aspect of the success of the new-model *formazione professionale*, I was told, was that it is provided by nonstate institutions that, thus, have much more discretion over the appointment of the most competent and appropriate staff, and other aspects of school management, than is the case with state secondary schools. In contrast with nonstate *scuole paritarie* receiving the *buono scuola* (school voucher), these vocational institutions are fully funded by the region. This creates a precedent for one of the policy innovations that I will recommend in the fourth section.

## 6.4. THE LOMBARD RESPONSE

Apart from the system of *formazione professionale*, the most significant instrument of the region with respect to implementing the principle of subsidiarity in general education is the *buono scuola*, now a part of the *dote scuola*.

There are about 7,000 schools in Lombardy, or 13.8 percent of the national total, serving a little more than a million pupils. Of these, 67.3 percent are state schools directly dependent upon the national ministry, while the balance are recognized nonstate schools, representing 19 percent of such *scuole paritarie* in Italy. The proportion of pupils in Lombardy attending nonstate schools is growing steadily, from 8.2 percent at the primary, 8.3 percent at the lower secondary, and 8.6 percent at the upper secondary in 2004–2005, to 8.6, 9.2, and 9.2 percent respectively three years later.

The primary instrument for regional influence on schools providing general education has been through grants and vouchers, recently brought together under the system of *dote*, which have greatly simplified administration and participation. Consistent with the principles of the centrality of the person, and of subsidiarity,

> La Regione oggi non finanzia i servizi attraverso contributi agli enti e ai soggetti che operano nella filiera di istruzione, formazione e lavoro, ma sostiene direttamente le persone, che hanno così possibilità di scegliere l'offerta che meglio risponde ai loro bisogni e alle loro scelte culturali[8]

> (Regione Lombardia Direzione Generale Istruzione, Formazione e Lavoro, 2010, p. 19).

Payments are made directly into the accounts of those eligible (by income criteria, in most cases, but also in some cases by handicap or by academic merit) before the start of the school year, thus enabling them to function with full dignity as clients choosing which services to select.

The most important aspect of this complex program for our purposes is the *Dote Scuola per l'Istruzione*. Its purposes are described as follows:

> Obiettivi: garantire la libertà di scelta delle famiglie e il diritto allo studio di ciascuno; sostenere le famiglie nelle spese relative alla frequenza scolastica; premiare il merito e l'eccellenza; alleviare i costi aggiuntivi sostenuti dagli studenti disabili che frequentano le scuole paritarie [that is, nonstate]; favorire la semplificazione e l'efficienza dell'azione amministrative e la tempestività nell'erogazione dei finanziamenti.[9]
>
> (Regione Lombardia Direzione Generale Istruzione, Formazione e Lavoro, 2010, p. 110)

In 2009–2010, 265,000 students in Lombardy, or 26 percent of the total, are benefitting from the *dote scuola*. Since the amount granted is related to actual costs, more funding is going to pupils in nonstate schools than to pupils in state schools, even though more of the latter receive benefits of some amount (see Table 6.1).

There are at least four respects in which this is a significant policy intervention:

1. it has enabled thousands of moderate-income families to exercise school choice in a manner that for many of them would not have been possible, thus putting the user of the service at the center (Interv. *Albonetti*);
2. it has provided resources and an incentive for schools to develop distinctive missions, responsive to an assessment by educators and parents of what is in the best interest of particular groups of pupils;
3. it has created a virtuous competition between state and nonstate schools to persuade parents that each provides a satisfactory education (thus consistent with the right to an "acceptable" education, as

**Table 6.1**   Beneficiaries and Amount Received

|  | State Schools | Nonstate School |
|---|---|---|
| Number of Beneficiaries | 198,113 (73%) | 72,904 (27%) |
| Amount Granted | €39,448,320 (39%) | €62,934,282 (61%) |

*Source*: The author's own elaboration on the basis of Regione Lombardia Istruzione, Formazione e Lavoro (2010) *Bilancio di Mandato: L'Istruzione, la Formazione, il Lavoro in Lombardia: Attività Risultati Innovazioni del Ottava Legislatura (2005–2010)*, p. 113.

defined by the UN Committee on Economic, Social and Cultural Rights);

4. it has helped the alternative nonstate schools to survive and flourish, thus giving real meaning to the principle of subsidiarity.

Admirable as the effects of this policy instrument have been, they have some definite limits. An obvious limit is that the size of the *dote* does not cover the full cost of attendance at a nonstate school, thus excluding the poorest families.

Another is that the leverage on state schools is limited, given that their primary funding comes by formula from the national government, especially in the form of teacher salaries, and given the detailed regulatory framework within which they are forced to function despite the legal principle of their autonomy.

Most damaging is that the *dote scuola* are an inadequate instrument to address the continuing weakness of the Italian education system, made up to an overwhelming degree of state schools. It is true that test results in Lombardy are significantly better than those for Italy as a whole. This comparative advantage—given that the state schools (*scuole statali*) in Lombardy function under the same conditions as schools elsewhere in the country—should be attributed largely to the well-known culture of hard work, initiative, and concern for results that characterize Lombardy. It is good, but not good enough.

What is required to provide a truly effective system of general education? There is a growing international consensus that at least three elements are required:

1. clear external standards for results aligned with curriculum and teacher training; the present state system of "profiles" of what should be accomplished in the two levels of schooling is, by all accounts, not aligned consistently with curriculum and assessment, while the region's own standards for schools are limited to noninstructional matters such as health and safety and thus do not provide leverage for improvement;

2. true autonomy—scope to create a coherent school team focused on a clearly articulated mission—at the school level; this is impossible in state schools in Italy, given especially the personnel policies that frustrate the creation of stable teams with a shared vision; the region has no authority in this area, though its partial support for nonstate schools helps to maintain an alternative system where such discretion does exist.

3. highly competent teachers working within a framework of account-ability; the national register (*elenco nazionale*) of teachers, from which assignments are made to state schools is established by the national ministry, and the region has no authority to determine the qualifications of teachers or to select those who work in state schools within Lombardy. That remains a serious hindrance to implementation, by legislation, of the provisions of Article 117 of the constitution.

In short, within the strict legal limits of its role, the region has ingeniously found ways to influence general education, including in state schools, through providing *dote scuola*, resources to enable those school directors with sufficient vision and leadership ability to take various measures to make their schools more effective and more attractive to parents. This "virtuous market" may, over time, lead to a general improvement of education as more and more schools take advantage of the extra resources and the pressure of parental choice to make effective use of the 25 percent of instructional time available for school-initiated activities.

It does not, however, go far enough.

## 6.5. Making Subsidiarity Real in Lombard Education

### 6.5.1. Regional Control

The most sensible and far-reaching basis for fundamental reform of general education in Lombardy would be for the region to press at the national level, in alliance with other progressive regions, for enabling legislation to implement the provisions of Section 117 of the 2001 Constitution for regional control of schools.

This is not a measure to be undertaken lightly, as is evident from the outcome of the Conferenza Stato/Regioni in 2003–2004. It would require careful advance planning, especially in three areas:

1. fiscal management;
2. personnel management and transfer from state to regional employment;
3. accountability for school and teacher performance (*valutazione*).

In addition, *it would not be a great improvement and would be contrary to the principle of subsidiarity if this were simply a measure of decentralization and in effect created a new regional bureaucratic structure answering to Milan in place of that answering to Rome.* The region should consider carefully how to implement the principle of subsidiarity in the management of a system of regional schools before seeking to create such a system.

Note that this recommendation is consistent with the agenda for the next five-year legislative period laid out by the region's director general for schools, training and labour, and discussed above.

## 6.5.2. Regional Teacher Force

A less radical measure would retain for now the present system of state control and civil service status for teachers, but would create a regional register (*elenco regionale*) of teachers in place of the present national register (*elenco nazionale*). Since teachers are already recruited and appointed through the regional offices of the national ministry, this would be relatively simple to administer. The advantage would be that the region, through cooperation with the universities, could seek over time to create a highly competent regional teaching force, and develop ways of recognizing and rewarding outstanding teachers and promoting their careers within the Lombard schools.

It could also lead to greater stability of the teaching force in schools in Lombardy, itself an important contribution to educational quality. The director general points out that, on average, 27 percent of the teachers in Lombardy are new to the schools where they teach each year. Ten percent of these are new teachers, which is high but not dramatically so by international standards, but the other 17 percent move around as a result of the personnel policies of the national ministry. I strongly endorse the director general's statement:

> Con l'attuazione del Titolo V [della Costituzione del 2001], le regioni avranno un ruolo nella contrattazione colletiva nazionale e regionale, e si potrà agire per ridurre la mobilità annuale degli insegnanti attraverso la revisione delle modalità di reclutamento, del contratto integrativo e l'introduzione de una priorità regionale per i trasferimenti.[10]

(Regione Lombardia Direzione Generale Istruzione, Formazione e Lavoro, 2010, p. 192)

## 6.5.3. Model Schools

Another feasible and powerful measure would take advantage of the region's greater leverage in relation to nonstate schools to create models of effective schools that, over time, could influence practices in other schools, in part through the choices made by parents.

The effect of parent choices promoted by the *dote scuola* would have the effect of forcing inadequate schools to close (Interv. *Albonetti*). While I believe that this may be overly optimistic, he is certainly thinking along the right lines.

The region could go beyond the present measures to provide full funding for selected nonstate schools, or full funding at least for pupils meeting family income criteria. These would have to be schools with strong leadership and staff willing to participate.

In exchange for this full funding, the region would set clear expectations for academic performance, and would require the schools to develop effective systems of teacher performance review, with negative as well as positive consequences.

The present policy of full funding for nonstate schools of *formazione professionale* provide a precedent for this recommendation.

Over time, the number of schools participating could increase naturally.

The experience gained through these two "partial" reforms would, of course, increase the capacity of the region eventually to implement the first and longer-term reform described above.

## 6.6. Conclusion

To sum up my impressions of general education in Lombardy in a few words, a population whose culture emphasizes hard work and a focus on results is forced to send its children to schools where "going through the motions" is apparently enough for many staff.

While, by all accounts, there are many competent and hardworking teachers in the state schools, by the same accounts there are many others who should not be entrusted with a classroom of children. Perhaps the most telling comment was made by a parent leader whom I asked why she had taken her child out of a state school. Reflecting a moment, she came out with two words: "*per caso.*" It was not that the state school was always bad, but that she could not have confidence that it would always be good, that her child would always have an adequate teacher. Another informant told me that parents were opposing the proposed change back to the single classroom teacher, since with three teachers each year there was a good chance that at least *one* of them would be competent.

Roberto Formigoni said, in his response to the report on the last five years of "Società, Governo e Sviluppo del Sistema Lombardo," that families were at the center of government concern in Lombardy, and would become even more so in the next years.

Families in Lombardy deserve better education for their children!

## NOTES

1. *Transl:* "The desire to be protected and supported by the State."
2. *Transl.:* "The Region, applying the principle of horizontal subsidiarity, recognizes and encourages citizens' autonomous initiatives, singularly and in associations, of families, social formations, and institutions, associations and civil and religious bodies, guaranteeing their contribution to the planning and realization of various public works and services."
3. *Transl.:* "In this way clear encouragement is given to active citizenship, where citizens, singularly or in associations, autonomously promote initiatives of general interest: initiatives that the Region, according to regional law, is then obliged to recognize, sustain, and, above all, include in its policies."
4. *Transl.:* "Contributions for the Ninth legislative period."
5. *Transl.:* "Redefine roles and functions in harmony with a national legislative context, which is undergoing profound change, and is now experiencing those greater responsibilities at the regional level that Lombardy has long been prepared for, and is ready to assume."
6. *Transl.:* "The process, which sees the Region as the key actor in policies for education and training, as per the reform of Article V of the Constitution, will receive new impetus from the full implementation of fiscal federalism. This line of development will be fully implemented in the IX legislature, which will gather the results of autonomy and self-responsibility of schools, freed from the current centralized and bureaucratic organization which limits their capacity to make proposals and innovations. The results of this process will reach full autonomy, meaning, first of all, to entrust institutions with their own economic management, to directly select personnel and be responsible for labour relations with staff, in order to administer resources more efficiently and give more importance to teachers, via recognition, also economic rewards, for length of service and merit. Autonomy and responsibility for schools does not entail reduced regional responsibilities. The Regional Government is an important actor not only to guarantee economic and financial sustainability but also to oversee and to control the program."
7. *Transl.:* "Sustain unity among the sections of society, the different territories, various economic and cultural voices, enhancing the differences and the characteristics of each reality, since cohesion does not mean homogenization but rather multiplication of opportunities for all."
8. *Transl.:* "The Regional Government today does not finance services via contributions to the bodies and subjects that operate in the field

of instruction, training and work, but rather directly sustains persons, who in this way can choose the supplier who best meets their needs and cultural choices."

9.  *Transl.*: "Objectives: to guarantee freedom of choice to families and the right to education for everyone, support families with school attendance costs; reward merit and excellence; alleviate the additional costs for disabled students who attend non-State schools; encourage simplification and efficiency of administration and timeliness in providing funds."

10. *Transl.*: "With the application of Article V [of the Constitution of 2001], the regions would have the role of negotiating national and regional collective contracts, and could then act to reduce the annual upheaval caused by teachers moving school via a revision of recruitment methods, supplementary contracts and introducing a regional priority for transfers."

## REFERENCES

Charnitzky, J. (1996) *Fascismo e scuola. La politica scolastica del regime (1922–1943)* (Florence: La Nuova Italia).

IReR (2009a) *Lombardy Region: Economic and Institutional Features, An Experience in Government* (Milan: IReR).

IReR (2009b) *Società, governo e sviluppo del sistema Lombardo: Lombardia 2010, rapporto di legislatura* (Milan: Guerini).

IReR, (2009c) *Lavoro e impresa: Lombardia 2010, rapporto di legislatura* (Milan: Guerini).

Malizia, G., and B. Stenco (1999) "Il cammino delle riforme tra razionalizzazione e libertà, tra efficienza ed eguaglianza" in *Scuola Cattolica in Italia* (Brescia: Editrice la Scuola).

Mauro, M. (1999) "La chiamano parità, ma per Mauro è un inaccettabile obolo" (from *Il Foglio*, July 24, 1999), in *Libertà, Libertà* (Milan: Tempi).

OHCHR website, http://www2.ohchr.org/english/law/cescr.htm, accessed on October 4, 2011.

Presidenza della Repubblica, *Regolamento recante norme in materia di autonomia delle istituzioni scolastiche, ai sensi dell'art. 21 della legge 15 marzo 1997, n. 59*, decree no. 275, 1999.

Regione Lombardia Direzione Generale Istruzione, Formazione e Lavoro (2010) *Bilancio di mandato: L'Istruzione, la formazione, il lavoro in Lombardia. Attività, risultati e innovazioni del'VIII legislatura (2005–2010)* (Milan).

Ribolzi, L. (1987) *Il falso dilemma pubblico-privato: L'anomalia della scuola italiana nel contesto europeo* (Turin: Fondazione Giovanni Agnelli).

Ribolzi, L. (2000) *Il sistema ingessato: autonomia, scelta e qualità nella scuola italiana* (Brescia: La Scuola).

UNHCHR website, http://www.unhchr.ch/tbs/doc.nsf/0/ae1a0b126d06 8e868025683c003c8b3b?Opendocument, accessed on October 4, 2011.

Valli, A. M. (1991) "Libertà per la scuola" in *Fogli*, 3–53.

# 7

# REGIONAL GOVERNANCE OF HEALTH
# SERVICES IN LOMBARDY

## *Helen Haugh*

## 7.1. INTRODUCTION

This chapter presents insights into the impact of subsidiarity-informed governance reforms introduced in Lombardy in 1995 (regional law no. 31/1997). This is achieved by exploring the impact of the governance reforms on the structure, services, and stakeholders in health services in the Lombard region. Secondary information about the governance reforms and an overview of health and social care was provided by the *Istituto Regionale di Ricerca della Lombardia* (IReR). Primary data were gathered in interviews with directors from the Lombard region and managers from public and private hospitals. Fieldwork was conducted during a visit to Lombardy in January 2010. The chapter concludes with my personal reflections on the impact and implications of the reforms for health services.

## 7.2. BACKGROUND CONTEXT

Historically, the states have always played a direct role in the economy of all European countries. Along with legislation and regulation, national governments have been responsible for the delivery of some services, for example, health, education, transport, and infrastructure. This mixed economy approach received a major boost in the welfare reforms introduced after 1945 and ultimately led to a model in which the state in some countries had a virtual monopoly to provide a prescribed list of services.

In the 1980s, the mixed economy model came under attack for several reasons: state involvement in large areas of service delivery was ideologically opposed by Conservative and right-wing political groups, which in some countries were in ascendancy; the increasing financial costs of delivering services was becoming increasingly difficult to fund from taxation; and the practical limitations of ensuring that large, bureaucratic public organizations were both effective and efficient. The result was new thinking in political economy that ultimately led to a reduction in the role of the state, a hollowing out (Rhodes, 1994), and the devolution of power and responsibilities away from the state to constellations of organizations and associations. The reforms were adopted in the UK, France, Belgium, Germany, the Netherlands, and Italy (Morel, 2007). In Italy, the reconfiguration of public sector governance involved an entire country embracing a new model of public administration that was inspired by the political theory of subsidiarity.

## 7.3. SUBSIDIARITY

Subsidiarity is defined as a "theory of social responsibility that recognizes the priority of the smallest units of society, while ensuring against interference from excessive government intervention" (Colombo and O'Sullivan, 2012, p. 37).

The philosophy of subsidiarity is rooted in the primacy of personal and interrelational responsibility above all other political powers and structures. In vertical subsidiarity there is an assumption of hierarchical relationships in which higher-level institutions serve to support, not replace, lower-level institutions. In horizontal subsidiarity the responsibility for jurisdictions, functions, and services is shared between different social actors in a nonhierarchical constellation. In practice this means that the state abandons the traditional administrative model of direct control of the delivery of services through a large public sector workforce and instead oversees and administers the delivery of services through contractual relationships with a network of different providers.

Underpinning subsidiarity is the principle that any authority should perform only those tasks that cannot be carried out effectively either by individuals or by private groups acting independently. The philosophy introduces the idea that different individuals and groups take on different roles according to their expertise. Subsidiarity is thus embedded in relationships between individuals and organizations. In vertical subsidiarity the relationships are hierarchical, and in horizontal subsidiarity they occur at the same level in the hierarchy.

In practice subsidiarity is associated with three characteristics: pluralistic supply; freedom of consumer choice (via accreditation of competing providers and conferring purchasing power on users) and fiscal autonomy (based on coupons, vouchers and endowments, and tax exemptions and allowances) (Brugnoli and Vittadini, 2009). However subsidiarity goes beyond privatization and contracting out to include increased participation of individuals in civil society to pursue the common good. The defining feature of the social relations between citizens is the mutual fulfillment of the goals of those participating in them (Colombo and O'Sullivan, 2012, p. 40).

The separation of commissioning from the provision of services creates a market place in which multiple organizations compete with each other to provide services. However, not all the rules of an open market apply and hence the term *quasi market* (Le Grand, 1990) was coined to describe the new structures. The separation of commissioning from service provision introduced competition into the quasi market of former public services. The belief is that competition would force providers to be both efficient and effective. In the main this is achieved by the widespread diffusion across the public sector of standard business and management tools and techniques, for example, strategic planning, cost control, and innovation management. To make the new system function, the management of former public services is coordinated through contractual relationships between agents and the regional government, which is both a supervisor and evaluator of agent performance (Colombo and O'Sullivan, 2012, p. 38).

This new political economy has been called governance (in contrast to government) and is characterized by the state acting as a regulatory instrument and not an agent of social action. Formal regulation and control is specified in the terms and conditions of contracts and agreements, and standards and accountabilities are maintained through linking pay to performance. Informally, however, it is inevitable that relationships impact on the mechanisms of subsidiarity. For example, when analyzing the implementation of the reforms in water and sanitation services in Italy, it became evident that regulation at the local level is more a matter of interpersonal and interinstitutional networks than of legal contracts and formally competitive interest relationships (Lippi et al., 2008). This chapter investigates subsidiarity in the Lombard region in policy area of health services.

## 7.4. GOVERNANCE REFORMS IN LOMBARDY

The rise of regionalism in Italy in the late 1970s led to Lombardy becoming an autonomous region by the 1990s. This status conferred formal regulatory powers on the region for a range of competences that had previously been maintained by the central state. The general framework for regional action is set by central government, whereas administrative and regulatory responsibility is devolved to the regions. In the beginning, fiscal powers were not devolved; however, fiscal federalism was approved in May 2009 and hence the region now has both power and responsibility to raise and administrate financial resources related to local competences.

Since 1995 the Lombard region has pursued a new model of governance inspired by the principle of subsidiarity. The regional government maintains the functions of regulating, programming, and financing while the management and delivery of services is shared between the public, private, or nonprofit organizations and associations. The change to a governance regime created an opportunity for radical change in the way that services were delivered. The reforms led to a reduction in size of regional executive and consolidation of legislation. Between 1995 and 2009 employment in regional administration was reduced from 600 to 250 executives and from 4,500 to 3,000 employees; and between 1995 and 2009 the laws were reduced from 2,000 to 500 through the creation of the Consolidation Acts.

## 7.5. REGIONAL GOVERNANCE AND HEALTH SERVICES IN LOMBARDY

Of the many responsibilities devolved from the centre to the regions, health care is perhaps the most significant as it accounts for the majority of government expenditure. For example, health-care costs account for more than 65 percent of expenditure by the regional government in Lombardy. The percentage of expenditure on health services as a proportion of gross domestic product (GDP) has risen continuously and this has been explained by demographic changes and technological innovation. The next section of this chapter provides an overview of the governance reforms in health care introduced in Lombardy after 1995.

In Lombardy, the public sector role in health services provision has been radically transformed from a classic monopoly of provision to a mixed economy of public, private, and third-sector organizations (Colombo, 2008; Colombo and O'Sullivan, 2012, p. 42). The reorganization of the regional health-care system was defined in laws no. 502/1997 and no. 517/1993 and regional law no. 31/1997.

The mainstay of the new governance system in health care in Lombardy is the *Aziende Sanitarie Locali* (ASLs) that were created to replace the former health authorities. ASLs are commissioning agents with responsibility for planning, accreditation, and quality control of providers of services and do not deliver any health services directly. They have been allowed some autonomy in the organization and management of their services to enable them to address specific problems and demands of their territories (Brugnoli and Vittadini, 2009, p. 30) however this has been bounded by strict financial requirements (Colombo and O'Sullivan, 2012, 42).

In the new governance system the region defines rules and standards of quality, approves the tariffs for treatments and medical procedures, issues contracts and authorizes reimbursement. Quality standards specify performance criteria, for example, maximum waiting times and the tariffs specify both technical procedure and reimbursement rates. The tariffs are the same for public, private, and nonprofit providers of services. However, there are specific tariff mechanisms that aim to reward, and thereby promote, virtuous structures that respond to public demands and penalize the less efficient. These rules of the market are administered by the ASLs.

ASLs have developed significant quality evaluation processes concerning the number and type of illnesses treated, which in turn are closely linked to the reimbursement system based on the *Diagnosis Related Groups* (DRGs) (Brugnoli and Vittadini, 2009, p. 36). The financing provided by the region for health-care structures is determined by more than five hundred DRGs. These medical networks are involved in tariff setting by providing information and advice about technical and other issues. For example, DRGs classify admissions to hospitals based on illness diagnosis to patients when discharged from hospitals. The DRGs calculate costs using data on diagnosis and resources needed during hospitalization (Brugnoli and Vittadini, 2009, p. 36). The calculations are based on metrics and do not take into account social costs, such as the quality of relationships between service providers and patients, and social outcomes.

For patients, the freedom to choose which providers to consult has conferred on them a new role as active citizens. This in turn has obliged them to exercise choice in an area in which they previously had none.

## 7.6.  Impacts of the Reforms

From a general perspective, the impact of the reforms can be observed in three areas. First, the transformation of the former USLs into ASLs created institutional change by introducing a new form of organization with responsibility for commissioning service delivery. The ASLs are also responsible for accreditation, monitoring, and control of the delivery of health services. This has required the creation of an inspection system, expertise in contracting, and mechanisms for reimbursing health service deliverers. In addition, the DRGs have been given responsibility for setting tariffs for medical procedures. These new responsibilities for the ASLs and the DRGs require employees to learn new knowledge and acquire new skills in order to create a functioning system. Second, the type of organizations involved in health service has expanded. Patient choice backed by financial reimbursement introduced aspects of competition into the economy of health care where none had previously existed. Existing hospitals became public limited companies wholly owned by their regional ASL. The flow of real money into the market for health care attracted new suppliers, for example, private and nonprofit organizations, that are in competition with the public sector hospitals. Third, the new market for health care in which patients are actively involved in making choices has changed the discourse of health care from a public service logic to a market place logic, albeit a quasi market with rules that differ from open markets (Le Grand, 1990). At this stage in the reforms, the impact of this may be too early to comment on but it is possible that in due course the market logic could drive out the shared public sector values of caring, service, and community orientation.

## 7.7. STRUCTURE

Subsequent to the reforms the architecture of the Lombard health service consists of ASLs (15), health-care and social-care districts (86), public hospitals, private hospitals, and some nonprofit organizations that are mainly involved in research. The distribution of services between and the availability of procedures from public and private hospitals is still in the process of finding equilibrium. Hospitals bid to the ASLs for the right to supply services and the market has not yet cleared. The presence of nonprofit organizations as suppliers of health services is low despite Lombardy having a highly developed civil society with a large representation of voluntary associations (3,500) and nonprofit organizations (600), social cooperatives (1,100) in the Lombard region (2009). This could be explained by the high capital costs of establishing and managing hospitals and clinics. However, the presence of nonprofit organizations is thought to be higher in the provision of domiciliary and social care (Interv. *Vignali*).

Nonprofit organizations meet the challenge of subsidiarity in terms of relationship building in that fundamental to their governance structures are the notions of trust and collective action (Weisbrod, 1988), and the norm of reciprocity (Gouldner, 1960). The nondistribution constraint (Hansmann, 1980) acts as a guarantor of the trustworthiness of the nonprofit organization in that it controls opportunistic behavior, prevents the misappropriation of resources, detracts from goal-displacement, and in doing so protects the reputation of the nonprofit governance structure as a socially responsible organization (Ben-Ner, 1986; Ortmann and Schlesinger, 2003; Steinberg, 2006).

Italy has been at the forefront of developments in business-oriented nonprofit organizations. In 1991, the social cooperative legal form was introduced. Italian social cooperatives are designed to enable economic activity to be aligned with social mission. In addition to holding shares in a social cooperative, local people are part of the governance structure of the social cooperative through membership of the governing board. Although stakeholder participation may reduce efficiency in decision making this should to be evaluated against the benefits of increased community stakeholder participation in local governance. In 2006, Italy introduced a Social Enterprise Law (155/2006) that defined the conditions of social enterprises: organizations performing an entrepreneurial activity of production of social benefit goods and services; 70 percent of total income must be reached through this main activity; the mission must be to provide social benefit and general-interest goals; there must be employees and a maximum of 50 percent voluntary workers. Social enterprises are thus business-oriented organizations with a social mission and have the potential to play an important role in the health service quasi market in Lombardy. In the UK, social enterprises have been encouraged at national level to bid for contracts to deliver public services (H. M. Treasury, 2002), and a unit within the National Health Service has been established to promote social enterprise within the health sector (Department of Health, 2008).

## 7.8. SERVICES

The Lombard governance reforms are driven by goals of achieving economy, efficiency, and effectiveness and impacts can be observed in the type, mode, and location of service delivery in Lombardy.

The introduction of tariffs has necessitated standardization of services and procedures in accordance with the tariff and reimbursement criteria. This policy ensures equality of services and procedures across different providers, however, it might constrain innovation as providers adhere to the specifications and quality standards. Although in practice, innovation in health care has continued to thrive, in the long term a balance will need to be found in order to ensure consistency in service delivery as well as incentivizing innovation.

Innovation has occurred in the mode of service delivery. Admissions to hospitals have fallen by 15 percent between 1995 and 2003 (IReR, 2005) and in the same period day hospital care has risen by 73 percent (IReR, 2005). Overnight hospital admission is costly and by increasing day admissions hospitals can reduce their costs. However, although financially expedient this approach to cost control must be rigorously monitored and evaluated to ensure that day care (in contrast to hospital admission) is in the best interests of patients.

There is potential for innovation in the location of service delivery. The market-based system has created opportunities for new providers to enter the market and the potential to scatter service provision across Lombardy. To achieve economies of skill and learning in medical procedures, centers of excellence in specific procedures may increase the cost effectiveness of the new health service economy in Lombardy. However, this is likely to impact on accessibility of services to patients located far away from a center of excellence.

To implement the tariff system service providers have been required to develop forecasting and budgeting skills. During the transition to the tariff-based payment system providers have maintained some flexibility in cost planning and budgeting and this has allowed room for innovation. As this tariff system becomes embedded in health service delivery, this flexibility is likely to be reduced unless provision is made to preserve flexibility and incentivize innovation.

## 7.9. STAKEHOLDERS

The impact of the reforms can be analyzed in relation to four different stakeholder groups. The separation of commissioning from provision of services conferred on ASLs the status of principals, and hospitals and other institutions became agents. To achieve efficiency and effectiveness public hospitals have been pushed into adopting business and management techniques that were developed in the private sector. The distinctive characteristics of the principles and value systems of the private and public sectors are different and so the direct transfer of techniques has not been without criticism. Private hospitals and nonprofit organizations are new agents and have learned the new rules of the health-care market and might shape future rules. Although physicians have reported increased job satisfaction they have seen their role expand from medical and surgical functions to include managerial responsibilities. Finally, although patients report high levels of satisfaction, these data refer to satisfaction with services and not in relation to their ability to exert freedom of choice.

## 7.10. REFLECTIONS

The introduction of a quasi market in health care in Lombardy has inevitably introduced aspects of both competition and risk. To conclude I offer eight points for reflection.

1. The focus on efficiency and effectiveness underpins the new governance of health care in Lombardy. Whereas in the past health service organizations were both purchasers and providers, the separation of functions and the institutional differences between purchasers and providers means that efficiency and effectiveness of principals and agents should be assessed separately. At present the ASLs accredit and inspect the providers, and a mechanism for evaluating the performance of the ASLs is not apparent in the new system. It is likely that different ASLs will have developed their skills for contracting, accreditation, monitoring, and ensuring patient freedom of choice to accommodate the needs of their local population. Opportunities to benchmark performance and share knowledge across the ASLs would, therefore, be both interesting and beneficial as the devolved governance system becomes established.

2. The market is the domain in which the forces of supply and demand interact and reach equilibrium. Consumers expect their need for health services to be satisfied and the region promises that their demands for health services will be met: the challenge for the ASLs and service providers is to ensure sufficient service availability in accessible locations for patients. At present the dynamics of the market to reach equilibrium between supply and demand are still being worked out. Weak control may lead to duplication of services. In the long run, if other regions follow the Lombard model, capacity that has been built up to meet current demand from outside the region is likely to be in excess.

3. The system of accreditation, tariffs, contracting, and reimbursement might lead to homogenization of services and procedures, and reduce the incentives to innovate. Contract-based service delivery may lead to short-term thinking and the tariffs may lead to a race to the bottom to cut the price of services and procedures that might ultimately be detrimental to patients. To maintain Lombardy at the forefront of innovation in health care, incentives to innovate and experiment in type, mode, and delivery of services

need to be built into the new health system as well as opportunities to share knowledge about innovations across the region.

4. The new system requires investment by individuals and organizations to learn new rules, acquire new skills, and is predicated on the willingness of health sector employees and the availability of and access to information. Although the long-term outcome will be increased specialized knowledge and technical expertise, the period of learning may encounter short-term information asymmetries that impact negatively on performance. The costs and incentives to learn and implement the new system should be transparent and incorporated into future education, career development, and continuous professional development activities for health sector employees.

5. The core principle of subsidiarity is the active participation of citizens in governance. At present the Lombard governance reforms appear to be strong on vertical subsidiarity but less strong on horizontal subsidiarity and active citizen participation. Subsidiarity involves the exercise of power and responsibility by citizens and their empowerment through closer engagement with elected representatives. It is in this capacity that the potential of nonprofit organizations, especially the citizen-oriented governance structures of social cooperatives, social enterprises, and community organizations, have much to offer to ensure that the Lombard reforms adhere to the philosophy of subsidiarity and not *quasi subsidiarity*. For example, patient councils and patient governors, as adopted in the UK, could strengthen subsidiarity by facilitating the flow of information between patients, service providers, and commissioners.

6. In addition to citizen empowerment through participation, nonprofit organizations have the further advantage that efficiency gains are ploughed back into the health system and not used to service dividend payments to shareholders.

7. The quasi market should ensure that the types of services delivered are responsive to demand. The ageing structure of the Lombard population is likely to require services that are more costly and more long term to deliver. Those services that are not well funded will be less attractive to provide and the burden of provision might fall in public sector hospitals that must carry the additional costs, thereby making a financially sustainable business model more difficult to achieve. This is especially relevant for health services that have a large care element that is not included in an economic costing model and therefore not likely to be of interest to private sector organizations.

8. Information systems have been created to manage the delivery of health care, and data on the costs, volume, and efficacy of treatments and procedures is being collected. This data is vital for forecasting demand and planning supply. Information could also be gathered about the impact of the reforms in terms of patient experience, and this would be useful for evaluating and improving the implementation of the reforms. Information on the emergence and sustainability of new organizations to deliver health services as well as their comparative strengths, weaknesses, and impacts on patient experience would be especially helpful for policy development to further embed the principles of subsidiarity in the Lombard region.

The planning, management, and administration of the governance reforms in Lombardy has radically changed both the structure and the institutional rules in the health services field. The separation of commissioning from provision is mediated through contractual relations, the terms of which are determined by the new governance structures and the tariffs for treatments and procedures. The administration of the new system has generated information about supply and demand and this can be used to improve the effectiveness and efficiency of the reforms.

## 7.11. Conclusion

The governance reforms in Italy created radical change in both the policy arena and implementation of health services in the Lombard region. The separation of commissioning from provision introduced competition and created a quasi market in health care. The reforms focus on ensuring service availability and were initiated centrally and implemented with regional variations. The future success of subsidiarity-informed governance reform in Lombardy will be influenced by active participation of citizens in partnership-based models that link supply with demand in strong relationships between commissioners, providers, and patients. The challenge for the Lombard region therefore is to embed subsidiarity, to make it durable and institutionally robust and supported by individuals and communities. Many of the reforms are modeled on the public sector reforms in the UK and a comparative study to investigate how the Lombard region might learn from the UK experience of institutional change in the health sector would provide valuable information as Lombardy seeks to continuously improve the quality and availability of health services to the region.

# References

Ben-Ner, A. (1986) "Nonprofit organizations: Why do they exist in market economies?" in S. Rose-Akerman (ed.), *The Economics of Nonprofit Institutions* (Oxford: Oxford University Press).

Brugnoli, A., and G. Vittadini (2009) *Subsidiarity: Positive Anthropology and Social Organization. Foundations for a New Conception of State and Market and Key Points of the Experience in Lombardy* (Milan: Guerini).

Colombo, A. (2008) "The 'Lombardy model': Subsidiarity-informed regional governance" in *Social Policy & Administration*, 42(2), 177–96.

Colombo, A., and T. O'Sullivan (2012) "The Lombardy region, economic and institutional features, an experience in government" in (ed. with A. Brugnoli) *Government, Governance and Welfare Reform. Structural Changes and Subsidiarity in Italy and Britain* (Cheltenham: E-Elgar) [forthcoming].

Department of Health (2008) "Social enterprise, making a difference: A guide to the right to request." (Leeds: Department of Health).

Gouldner, A. W. (1960) "The norm of reciprocity: A preliminary statement" in *American Sociological Review*, 25(2), 161–78.

Hansmann, H. (1980) "The role of non-profit enterprise" in *Yale Law Journal*, 89(2), 835–98.

H. M. Treasury (2002) *The Role of the Community and Voluntary Sector in Service Delivery: A Cross Cutting Review* (London: Her Majesty's Treasury).

IReR (2005) *Studi per la predisposizione sulla Lombardia e sulle politiche regionali. Dossier sanità* (Milan: Guerini).

Le Grand, J. (1990) "Quasi-markets and social policy" in *The Economic Journal*, 101, 1256–67.

Lippi, A., N. Gianelli, S. Profeti, and G. Citroni (2008) "Adapting public-private governance to the local context. The case of water and sanitation services in Italy" in *Public Management Review*, 10(5), 619–40.

Morel, N. (2007) "From subsidiarity to 'free choice': Child- and elder-care reforms in France, Belgium, Germany and the Netherlands" in *Social Policy and Administration*, 41(6), 618–37.

Ortmann, A., and M. Schlesinger (2003) "Trust, repute and the role of the non-profit enterprise" in H. Anheier and A. Ben-Ner (eds.), *The Study of the Non-Profit Enterprise* (New York: Kluwer Academic).

Rhodes, R. A. W. (1994) "The hollowing out of the state: The changing nature of the public service in Britain" in *The Political Quarterly*, 65(2), 138–51.

Steinberg, R. (2006) "Economic theories of non-profit organizations" in W. W. Powell and R. Steinberg (eds.), *The Nonprofit Sector Research Handbook* (New Haven: Yale University Press).

Weisbrod, B. A. (1988) *The Non-Profit Economy* (Cambridge: Harvard University Press).

# 8

# SUBSIDIARITY, PROXIMITY, AND INNOVATION

## *Michael Kitson*

## 8.1. INTRODUCTION

The importance of developing regional innovation is prominent in the policy discourse throughout the European Union. Increasingly, however, the notion of innovation that is used is too narrow: with a focus on R&D, high-technology manufacturing, and the commercialization of science (Christopherson et al., 2008). These are important parts of the innovation system but they are not a complete picture—and often exclude wider forms of innovation. A more complete picture of innovation in a knowledge-based regional economy would include the development of innovative products and processes; innovation in business practices; innovation outside of the manufacturing sector—including knowledge-intensive business services and the public and third (nonprofit) sectors; and the important role of universities and hospitals as regional economic actors and sources of knowledge. This broader notion of "total innovation" puts an emphasis on networks, cooperation, people interactions, and local governance. This indicates that Lombardy is well placed to increase its innovation performance building on its history of cooperation and local governance as portrayed and emphasized by subsidiarity. The future challenges are to extend and build new networks and to document and analyze the extent of "total innovation" in the region.

This chapter is organized as follows: section 1 briefly considers the characteristics of the regional economy; section 2 argues for the importance of considering a wide notion of innovation—not just R&D and high-technology manufacturing; section 3 considers the importance for collaboration to promote innovation in the Lombard economy; section 4 considers the role of universities in the Lombard economy; section 5 considers some of the initiatives that may promote innovation in the region; and the final section, section 6, concludes by arguing that a form of governance based on subsidiarity is appropriate for promoting regional innovation, prosperity, and well-being.

## 8.2. THE LOMBARD ECONOMY

The Lombard economy is historically strong and contributes significantly to the overall level of prosperity in Italy. The region has a broad industrial structure but as with other advanced economies it is dominated by services, particularly in the Milan area. As part of an integrated and globalized economy, the region is subject to external shocks such as the current world financial crisis. Lombardy, however, is a "resilient region" as it can absorb shocks and ensure that they do not cause lasting impacts on the region's economy and society. Thus, the impact of the current negative shock has not been transmitted to a significant increase in unemployment (compared to many other parts of Europe).

This reflects the culture, norms, and behavior prevalent in the regions. Firms are reluctant to reduce their labor force in responses to an economic downturn. This reflects a number of motives, such as the need to maintain local networks and preserve the employment status of family and other members of the local community; as well as the concern that a loss of workers would lead to a loss of competences and knowledge that would be difficult to reacquire in the long term. The region's economy is highly dependent on small and medium-sized enterprises, and has relatively few large companies. This could create potential competitiveness problems if large firms have a competitive advantage due to the ability to exploit economies of scale and the ability to enter global markets. Many firms in the region have compensated for the size or aggregation problem by using networks to collaborate and/or by competing in niche markets. An important factor that will drive competitiveness in the future is how the region deals with intensified global competiveness and how it forges new forms of collaboration to increase its innovation performance.

## 8.3. THE IMPORTANCE OF TOTAL INNOVATION

It has been increasingly recognized that innovation is important in generating increased growth and improved welfare. The problem has been how to define what innovation entails—as it is a fuzzy and ill-defined concept. At the most basic level innovation has been defined as "the successful exploitation of new ideas" (DIUS, 2008, p.12). But innovation can vary in terms of products, services, processes, and business practices and it takes place in the private, public, and third sectors. The current focus of innovation policy, at local, regional, national, and international levels is based on the application of technology in the manufacturing sector. Policy initiatives tend to support R&D and mechanisms to support technology transfer from universities. There is an emphasis on the development of new technologies (e.g., information and communications technology (ICT) and biotechnology) and not the diffusion of existing technologies. These initiatives support important parts of the innovation system but they are partial and incomplete as they fail to address many aspects of "hidden innovation" that takes place in traditional sectors and in services—as well as in the public and third sectors.

Much of the focus on new technologies is concerned with the development of new general purpose technologies (GPTs), which are major advances in innovation that may have significant impacts on the economy and society. The development of ICT is considered as a recent example of a GPT and earlier examples include the steam engine, electricity, and the internal combustion engine.

Much of public policy, at both national and regional scales has focused on technologies that may have the potential to become GPTs. In the long term, GPT can have a major economic and social impact. But the impact of the GPT production on its own, only has a small economic impact as such technology producing sectors are small in terms of both employment and shares of gross domestic product (GDP) (Solow, 2001).This is particularly important when considered at the regional or local level, as the development and encouragement of "high-technology" clusters. However GPTs have a significant indirect effect: it is the use of GPTs that has the biggest impact on the economy. Thus, it is the use and the diffusion of ICT that has had a major recent impact on the growth in many advanced countries. It is important to note that the diffusion of technologies takes considerable time and requires the appropriate diffusions channels (such as networks) and appropriate level of public policy support.

Another distinction that can be made is between radical and incremental innovations. Radical innovations, which may evolve from GPTs, involve the development of a new product or service that incorporates major technological, process, or organizational changes.

Incremental innovations involve development along an existing technology or innovation trajectory. Incremental innovations can also be disaggregated according to whether they are new to the industry or the operating market of the firm, or just new to the firm. Furthermore we can consider the notion of "wider innovation," which includes development in management practices and organizational change. It is important to emphasize that the drivers, impact, and policy implications of different types of innovation will vary across sectors and across regions (Abreu et al., 2007).

It has been recently emphasized that much innovation involves interactions between different partners and organizations, as opposed to being developed by single research teams or in one corporate laboratory (Chesbrough, 2003; von Hippel, 1988). Thus, tapping into the research and expertise being conducted outside the company is vital including other firms, institutions, and customers. The recent emphasis on open and user-led innovation provides interesting insights and implications. First, accessing external knowledge may be difficult and costly. Second, the use of external knowledge does not alleviate the need for internal capacity to absorb, assimilate, and exploit such knowledge.

Overall, we can conceptualize innovation as being a broad process that takes place in a range of sectors and different parts of the economy and society. This notion of "total innovation" has a number of spatial and nonspatial implications.

One of the most important is the importance of "proximity" or "closeness" in a variety of dimensions or domains.

First, there is the importance of geographic proximity. If partners and collaborators are physically close to each other they are able to reduce transaction and transport costs and are able to talk and communicate effectively. Second, is the related concept of relational proximity. This is the notion that when individuals or groups have strong relational ties this generates trust and other forms of social capital that facilitate the exchange of knowledge and expertise. Knowledge comes in many different forms—a simple distinction is between codified and tacit knowledge. Whereas codified knowledge is easy to transfer or exchange, codified knowledge consists of norms, routines, and competence that require intense interactions to be shared and exchanged. Third, the development of ICT has facilitated the development of digital proximity, which can promote relational proximity (in the absence of geographical proximity) and the exchange of knowledge (of all types). Fourth, is the importance of governance proximity where governance mechanisms are close to the people or organizations that they are helping.

## 8.4. COLLABORATION AND INNOVATION IN LOMBARDY

Collaboration has been an important feature of the Lombard economy. In particular, parts of the regional economy have been characterized by industrial districts—geographically proximate clusters of SMEs, often in traditional sectors, that engaged in high levels of collaboration and experienced strong economic growth (Lazersona and Lorenzoni, 1999; Muscio, 2006). The notion of an industrial cluster can be traced back to Alfred Marshall, the Cambridge economist. Marshallian industrial districts were a concept based on a pattern of organization common in late nineteenth century Britain, where firms concentrating on the manufacture of specific products were geographically clustered (Marshall, 1890). The characteristics of a Marshallian industrial district include high degrees of vertical and horizontal specialization and the notion that there was "something in the air," which many have considered to mean knowledge spillovers— such as the exchange of tacit knowledge as discussed above.

The success of Italian industrial districts was one of the factors that encouraged policymakers across the world to adopt "cluster-based" policies to promote regional innovation and economic growth. The most prevalent promoter of the "cluster concept" is Michael Porter who argues that regional competitive advantage is based on the dynamics of geographically localized activities that are "geographic concentrations of interconnected companies, specialized suppliers, service providers, firms in related industries, and associated institutions (for example universities, standards agencies, and trade associations) in particular fields that compete but also co-operate" (Porter, 1998, pp. 197–98).

A problem with the Porter approach is that it is largely based on mapping where firms are located and not analyzing how firms behave. Clusters can take many forms and develop due to many different drivers. Furthermore just because firms are colocated does not mean that they are competing or collaborating with one another.

The Porter view of the cluster concept is largely an extension of the American neoliberal model of competitiveness and diverges from the Italian model. The Italian industrial district is not solely concerned with competiveness but reflects the historical, social, and cultural characteristics of the local economy. A number of scholars have emphasized that the strength of industrial districts is built around a strong commitment to the local community (Brusco, 1982; Piore and Sabel, 1984). This bottom-up approach to economic and social development emphasizes the need for local governance as epitomized by subsidiarity.

The characteristics of an effective industrial district include cooperative norms and structures; an adaptive and dynamic system; skilled labor; access to finance—often from local credit markets; effective local governance; strong local identity; and capacity to innovate. The latter is helped by stability in employment such that the introduction of technical or organizational change is not considered as threat to workers. The traditional industrial district has been characterized by geographical concentration. There have, however, been the development of new "meta-districts" that are evolving to promote the growth of new technologies.

Often these districts are not geographically proximate but they depend on many of the other virtues of traditional industrial districts—in particular relational proximity and trust. This often requires new mechanisms to build connectivity—such as through virtual or digital proximity. Such connectivity will often be sources of ideas outside of the region (and outside of the country), and will require effective cooperation with universities and other institutions from the science base (Abreu et al., 2007 and 2010).

Despite the history of successful collaboration in Lombardy there are many firms in the region—especially in services—that are disconnected. These are firms that are reluctant to cooperate because they are too small (the aggregation problem) or they lack the knowledge and competences to collaborate—they do not know how to do it, who with, or what the benefits may be. These problems of lack of connectivity and lack of information indicate the need for policy intervention to help create cooperative structures and networks that can build connectivity and improve the flow of information.

## 8.5. Innovation in Lombardy: The Role of Universities

The competitive challenges in developing a knowledge-based economy have been brought into sharp focus by the financial crises and the ensuing global recession. Globalization has put increasing pressure on many local communities as the paces of global competitive pressures accelerate. And much of the response to globalization has to be local—including developing human capital, building networks, and a collaborative economy. The ability of businesses within the local economy to adapt to new market, strategic, and technological opportunities is central to local growth and prosperity. And at the center of many local economies are universities—who are important employers, educators, and sources of ideas (Kitson et al., 2009).

Also, importantly universities do not tend to move—this they act as important local economic anchors—as well as "talent magnets" that can attract other skilled workers and businesses. There are many examples of universities being important sources of local economic growth—such as the role of Stanford University in contributing toward the "silicon valley" phenomenon, and of MIT and the other Boston universities toward the economic dynamism of Route 128. In Europe, the "Cambridge phenomenon" refers to the growth of the high-tech economy in Cambridgeshire, UK, which has been fostered in various ways by the presence of a world-class university—from licensing intellectual property and creating spinout companies, through to providing well-educated graduates and undertaking commissioned research and consultancy (Wicksteed, 1985). It is important to analyze the various ways in which knowledge is transferred from universities to the regional economy. It is important to recognize the different roles that individual universities play in their local and regional economies (Lester, 2005). This diversity will reflect a university's particular strengths and local economic trajectories. The form and nature of university-industry relationships and their impact on regional economies indicate that place, institutionally specific actors and local culture are important and they need to be considered within a wider context of total innovation.

Lombardy has many top-class universities who are important sources of talent and ideas. But there are a number of areas where their contribution to the regional economy could be strengthened. First, attracting more overseas students—having skilled labour with diverse backgrounds can help contribute to the knowledge base of the local economy—can stimulate interactions and help create a "buzz" (Storper and Venables, 2004), which is a characteristic of dynamic local economies. Second, the process of knowledge exchange between universities in the region and businesses and other sectors is not systematic but random with pockets of excellence and the matching between business strengths and research strengths being erratic. This is an area where policy can contribute to the building of networks or "innovation districts," which would be communities of businesses, universities, and the public and third sectors.

## 8.6. Strengthening the Local Innovation System

As discussed above "proximity" of various forms—including governance—are important parts of the innovation process. For some parts of the local economy geographic proximity has been important—this can be improved by developments in the transport system although this is, of course, very expensive.

Often geographic proximity has been important as it generates relational proximity, which builds trust and mutual understanding. Often, geographic proximity can be replaced by virtual proximity through the use of ICT. This requires help, advice, and information on the appropriate technologies and their diffusion.

Relational proximity can also be enhanced by developing institutions that support cooperation, network building, and "boundary spanning" (including between businesses and universities). This would require the development a secretariat that would provide network support functions. This secretariat would need to staffed with people with specialist skills (skills that may need to be developed)—in particular people who understand the needs and motivations of business, universities, and other partners in the innovation district. This initiative could include development or merger of existing institutions. It is important, in the spirit of subsidiarity, to emphasize that such a secretariat would not direct or control the partners in the district but it would help to maintain and "lubricate" the system.

There are a number of factors that need to be considered when building networks that promote cooperation. First, they must be flexible and able to adapt to prevent the emergence of institutional rigidity. Second, they must be open with ease of access to prevent the danger of barriers to entry. Third they must be outward and not inward looking—many ideas and insights will be from outside of the region. Fourth, it is important understand where there may be gaps or weakness in the value chain so that networks can focus where they will the largest impact.

## 8.7. CONCLUSION

Local economies are increasingly being influenced by global forces as shown by the impact of the financial crisis and the rise of China and other newly industrialized nations. But paradoxically this requires a greater focus on regions as the impact of globalization will be local and many of the necessary response will also be local.

For advanced regions, like Lombardy, future prosperity will depend on the further development of its knowledge-based economy—in an increasingly globalized world economy, advanced regions cannot compete on the basis of low-cost mass production. Instead they must exploit skills, ideas, networks, and the use of local assets (including universities and hospitals). And this requires a high degree of local interactions. Ideas are most effectively exchanged and exploited through people communicating with one another, as most knowledge is "tacit" and is held by people and is not "codified." And the exchange and use of knowledge requires trust—and this is developed by the encouragement of civic engagement, a strong local identity, and a sense of being part of a community.

It is vital to consider the appropriate governance mechanisms that can deliver innovation and local prosperity. This cannot be effectively delivered by top-down directives; instead it requires connectivity, responsiveness, and accountability to the local community. The Lombard model of subsidiarity provides the appropriate approach to governance, as it responsive to the needs of the local community and can ensure the best future direction for the local economy and the local community. The benefits of the approach is that vertical subsidiarity ensures that decisions are made at the lowest appropriate level and horizontal subsidiarity ensures that decisions are made at the nearest appropriate level.

The types of initiatives that would benefit from this approach would be the development of "innovation districts," which would build and help to maintain networks to promote collaboration and knowledge exchange between businesses, universities, and other actors from the public and third sectors. Such innovation districts would require people with specialist skills and knowledge to help foster collaboration between partners with different motives and competences. To promote innovation in the region some further research is required. First, a better understanding of the level of total innovation in the region—the conventional metrics such as expenditure on R&D do not adequately reflect the level of innovation. Second, an analysis of the extent and potential for innovation in the public and third sectors.

Finally, although the focus of this chapter has been on innovation and economic growth it is important to emphasize that subsidiarity is not only an appropriate approach to delivering prosperity. It is important in supporting and delivering the broader needs of a community, of which economic performance is just one part.

It is not simply about economic growth but about the quality of life—and, of course, the latter can be improved by innovation. Subsidiarity is important in engaging and responding to the local community to ensure that health, education, and environmental protection reflect the needs of the whole community—including variations in needs within the local community. In addition, it is important that the local community feels engaged and connects not only with the public sector but also the business and third (nonprofit) sectors.

# References

Abreu, M., V. Grinevich, M. Kitson, and M. Savona (2007) *Absorptive Capacity and Regional Patterns of Innovation* (London: DIUS).

Abreu, M., V. Grinevich, M. Kitson, and M. Savona (2010) "Policies to enhance the 'hidden innovation' in services: Evidences and lessons from the UK" in *The Service Industries Journal*, 30, 99–118.

Brusco, S. (1982) "The Emilian model: Productive decentralisation and social integration" in *Cambridge Journal of Economics*, 6, 167–84.

Chesbrough, H. W. (2003) *Open Innovation: The New Imperative for Creating and Profiting From Technology* (Cambridge MA: Harvard Business Press).

Christopherson, S., M. Kitson, and J. Michie. (2008) "Innovation, networks and knowledge exchange" in *Cambridge Journal of Regions, Economy and Society*, 1, 165–73.

DIUS (2008) *Innovation Nation* (London: DIUS).

Kitson, M., J. Howells, R. Braham, and S. Westlake (2009) *The Connected University: Driving Recovery and Growth in the UK Economy* (London: NESTA).

Lazersona, M. H., and G. Lorenzoni (1999) "The firms that feed industrial districts: a return to the Italian source" in *Industrial and Corporate Change*, 8, 235–66.

Lester, R. K. (2005) "Universities, innovation, and the competitiveness of local economies: a summary report from the local innovation systems project—phase i" in *MIT Industrial Performance Center Working Paper* (Cambridge, MA: MIT).

Marshall, A. (1890) *Principles of Economics* (London: Macmillan).

Muscio, A. (2006) "Patterns of innovation in industrial districts: An empirical analysis" in *Industry and Innovation*, 13(3), 291–312.

Piore, M. J., and C. F. Sabel (1984) *The Second Industrial Divide: Possibilities for Prosperity* (New York: Basic Books).

Porter, M. E. (1998) *On Competition* (Cambridge, MA: Harvard Business School Press).

Solow, R. (2001) "Information technology and the recent productivity boom in the US" in Cambridge–MIT National Competitiveness Summit (Cambridge, UK.).

Storper M., and A. J. Venables (2004) "Buzz: Face-to-face contact and the urban economy" in *Journal of Economic Geography*, 4, 351–70.

von Hippel, E. (1988) *The Sources of Innovation* (New York: Oxford University Press).

Wicksteed, Segal Quince (1985) *The Cambridge Phenomenon* (Cambridge: Segal Quince Wicksteed).

# 9

# Social Housing and Subsidiarity in the Lombard Model of Governance

*Gerard Van Bortel*

## 9.1. Introduction

This chapter discusses the Lombard social housing sector, and is structured as follows: Section 1 is a short description of the Italian and Lombard social housing sector, placing it in an international perspective and discussing the main challenges. Section 2 presents the key elements of the Lombard model of governance. These elements are placed in a public management framework to clarify the different coordination mechanisms that can underpin societal governance, that is, coordination by the state, market, community, and civil society (Brandsen et al., 2005). This section continues with a more detailed discussion of the different elements of subsidiarity-inspired governance in Lombard social housing practices. The chapter concludes with recommendations on the further implementation of subsidiarity in Lombard social housing. This chapter is based on desk research and a series of interviews conducted in 2009 with key actors in the Lombard social housing sector.

## 9.2. Social Housing in Italy and the Lombard Region in an International Perspective

### 9.2.1. Social Housing in Italy

Social housing in Italy makes up around 5 percent of total housing stock and less than 20 percent of rental housing (Federcasa, 2008). See Figure 9.1 for an international comparison. Traditionally, Italian

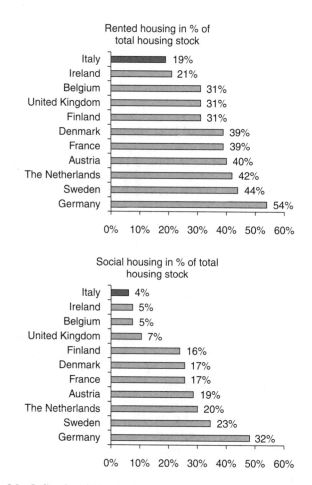

**Figure 9.1** Italian Social Housing in an International Perspective
*Source*: Housing Statistics in the EU, 2010.

social housing has never been object of significant state intervention. The first forms of social housing were created from about 1850 onward by housing cooperatives. In the twentieth century the state created a social housing sector exclusively for families that were not able to meet their housing needs via the open market. Consequently, Italian social housing was thereby separated from the regular for-profit housing market.

Based on Kemeny's 1995 work on housing, Italy can be classified as a dualist housing system. In unitary housing systems, such as the Netherlands, Germany, and Sweden, social housing is not separated from for-profit housing by distinctive legal and regulatory frameworks; rather the two forms of housing can compete with each other and, importantly, access to social housing is not restricted to low-income households. The Housing chapter of the *Lombardy 2010* report mentions that Lombardy still has a dualist system but is evolving to a more unitary system (IReR, 2009a).

## 9.2.2. Social Housing in Lombardy

Social housing in Lombardy can be divided into two categories: housing provided by cooperatives (mainly owner-occupied housing) and public housing owned by the region or the municipalities. Housing developed with subsidies from the Lombardy Regional Government can be divided into three segments:

1. *Canone Sociale*/public housing intended for the lowest income groups with a 80 percent of building costs subsidized by the region on building cost, built on municipal land earmarked for public services;
2. *Canone Moderato*/affordable housing for low- to middle-income households, with 40 percent regional subsidies. This type of housing is provided by *Azienda Lombarda per l'Edilizia Residenziale* (ALER), local authorities, and housing cooperatives;
3. *Canone Convenzionato*/subsidized housing for rental or purchase at prices below market level. This is supported with a 1.5 percent regional subsidy on interest rates.

### 9.2.2.1. Public Housing

Public housing is a means-tested form of housing intended for households with an annual income of less than €19,000. In Lombardy there are two types of public housing providers: regional housing managed by the Lombard Residential Building Company—ALER and municipal housing (see Table 9.1).

Approximately two-thirds of the 1,125 municipalities in Lombardy have social housing, one-third does not. Their public housing stock is mainly managed by the municipalities and, in some cases, management is outsourced to private or nonprofit actors. With 26,000 housing units the municipality of Milan is the biggest municipal landlord and outsources its housing management.

**Table 9.1**   Indicators on Housing Owned by Public Actors in Lombardy

| Indicator | Value |
|---|---|
| Percentage of communities with social housing | 64% |
| Total number of publicly owned social housing in Lombardy | 162.882 |
| • municipalities | 61.573 owned |
| | 19.413 managed |
| • regional housing organization ALER | 101.309 owned |
| | 112.167 managed |
| Social housing typologies: | |
| • Canone Sociale | 93% |
| • Canone Moderato | 1% |
| • Canone Convenzionato | 5% |
| • Liberomercato | 1% |
| Unoccupied housing | 18.525 |
| Rent Income | |
| • due rent income in 2006 | €127.270.341 |
| • defaults in 2006 | €22.741.332 |
| • accumulated defaults | €72.531.116 |
| Service charges income | |
| • due service charges income in 2006 | €72.695.607 |
| • defaults in 2006 | €7.856.044 |
| • accumulated defaults | €14.750.437 |

*Source*: The author's own elaboration on the basis of *Osservatorio regionale sulla condizione abitativa*, 2006.

### 9.2.2.2. Affordable Housing

A second type of social housing emerged after the responsibility for housing policy was devolved from the state to the regions. The target group for this *moderate*-priced rented housing (*canone moderato*) is broader and includes households with an annual income below €40,000. This new form of housing was created to support households that are excluded from public housing but still face difficulties in finding an affordable home.

### 9.2.2.3. Subsidized Housing

A third form of affordable housing comes in the form of subsidized rents. The Lombard region introduced this initiative in 2005 following a proposal from the housing cooperatives. This program is open to ALER, municipalities, cooperatives, nonprofit organizations, and private actors. The region gives a discount of 1.5 percent on the interest rates for loans needed to build the projects. The municipality needs to provide the land for these projects at no cost. The region allocated a €40 million annual budget to support this sacc-program (*Servizi Abitativi a Canone Convenzionato*).

At the outset SACC was intended only to encourage the availability of rented homes, but due to the low uptake by private actors, the program was adapted in 2008 to also include a form of deferred owner-occupied housing: properties are rented out for a period of eight years, after which it can be sold.

### 9.2.2.4. Social Housing Allocation

To receive government subsidies, housing developments must follow regional housing allocation rules. Housing waiting lists are managed by the municipalities based on criteria laid down by the regional government in a Housing Allocation Code. Households are given priority on the housing waiting list according to their ISEE score (*Indicatore Situazione Economica Equivalente*); this indicator is based not only on income but also on the social and economic situation of households, such as the number of family members.

Most housing cooperatives are reluctant to take part in government-subsidized programs, because this would force them to comply with regional allocation regulations; therefore they prefer to develop owner-occupied housing for their members.

### 9.2.2.5. Social Housing and Spatial Planning

Lombard legislation defines social housing as a "public service." This implies that social housing can be constructed on land that in local statutory planning has been zoned for public services. Social housing does not need to be built on areas zoned specifically for that purpose. This planning strategy is also influenced by the hesitance (and the not-in-my-backyard attitude) of many municipalities to designate land for social housing; as we have noted, a third of municipalities in Lombardy provide no rented social housing.

### 9.2.2.6. Regional Program for Social Housing

The Lombard regional social housing program (prerp, *Programma Regionale per l'Edilizia Residenziale Pubblica*) received €600 million over a period of three years (€200 million in 2007, 2008, and 2009) and contained two policy goals: to support demand and to support supply.

The demand pillar assists tenants to buy their home or receive financial assistance to pay the rent. The supply pillar redevelops estates by renovation or demolition, and builds new homes (aqst, *Accordi Quadro di Sviluppo Territoriale*). New home building targets were set for all three forms of housing, for example, social-, moderate-, and affordable-priced housing (SACC). Contracts to access the regional financial support are drafted on a provincial level and bring together actors such as ALER, municipalities, and cooperatives.

### 9.2.3. Social Housing Investment Funds

A relatively new form of affordable housing has come on stream with the *Fondazione Housing Sociale* (FHS) in Milan. This is an organization linked to the Cariplo Foundation, an ethical banking organization. FHS has attracted funding of €80 million; €10 million from the region and the rest from the ethical banking foundation and other investors. The housing developed by organizations like FHS is destined for medium-income households. The *joint property investment fund* is central to this form of affordable housing; it's an instrument particularly suited to social housing initiatives, providing a robust structure for defining and managing public and private interests.

A property fund is made up of autonomous capital divided into shares of the same value (with the same rights), owned by several investors and managed by an asset management company, which invests it exclusively, or predominantly in real estate or holdings in real estate companies. The property fund is supervised by the Bank of Italy and employs well-constructed governance arrangements. Advisory committees ensure that investors can express their views on the asset management company's strategy. The involvement of independent experts and auditors provide further checks and balances (Urbani and Van Bortel, 2009). The fund is rendered more flexible by regulatory constraints on selecting investments based on ethical and sustainability criteria. These measures safeguard the public interest requirements of the initiatives.

Although the concept of joint property funds is a promising avenue for more affordable housing units aimed at medium-income households, the road from this idea to start up of the first project has been long; the first social housing project developed by FHS using a property fund will probably come on the market in 2011.

### 9.3. SUBSIDIARITY, THE LOMBARD MODEL OF GOVERNANCE

Subsidiarity is the leading principle in the Lombard model of governance (Brugnoli and Vittadini, 2009). This model is based on a well-developed, well-described and mature political philosophy about how governance should be organized. The implementation of this model has been a priority of the regional government (which has held office continuously since 1995), and appears to be widely embraced by civil society and private actors. There is also a more pragmatic reason to adopt subsidiarity as the leading governance principle, simply because governments often do not have the knowledge or the resources to tackle societal problems (Koppenjan and Klijn, 2004). In addition, veto-power can easily stop government initiatives in countries with a well-developed civil society and powerful grassroot organizations.

### 9.3.1. Key Elements of Subsidiarity

This section describes if, and in what form, the following four key elements of subsidiarity (IReR, 2009b) can be found in Lombard social housing policy:

1. Vertical subsidiarity;
2. Horizontal subsidiarity;
3. Responsibility;
4. Quasi markets.

#### 9.3.1.1. Vertical Subsidiarity

Vertical subsidiarity is the principle that higher levels of government should not substitute the power and responsibility of lower ones if the functions can be adequately and effectively carried out at a lower level of government or by communities. Secondly, higher-level government institutions must assist the lower-level ones as needed, but only to the extent that they are unable to fulfill their assigned functions (IReR, 2009b). The devolution of the responsibility for housing policy from the national level to the regions in 1998 is a good example of vertical subsidiarity.

This devolution process took more than a decade. The financial provision and planning responsibilities have been gradually devolved to the regions, together with the functions concerning social housing. The main changes are around special funding exclusively for housing provision, and the central power's role in redistributing the resources among the regions.

In 2000, the region of Lombardy formally took over responsibility for public housing and the control of ALER, the organization responsible for managing the housing stock owned by the region. The president of ALER is appointed by the president of the region.

Every province in Lombardy has an ALER branch, the size of which differs from province to province; the Milan branch manages around 75,000 dwellings.

Ironically, the devolution of responsibility for housing policy from a national to a regional level appears to have decreased autonomy for ALER; while housing was the responsibility of the state, ALER had a lot of autonomy because the supervisors where far away in Rome, whereas currently the region has more control over the activities and governance of ALER.

ALER is criticized by some for its lack of efficiency. The absence of a clear asset management strategy has led to the sale of dwellings to tenants, eroding the social rental stock. This has also led to mixed rental/owner-occupied estates that make maintenance more complex and costly. The ALER-branches in cities often operate with an annual operating loss. The region, the taxpayer, and tenants, directly or indirectly, have to bear the consequences of these financial losses.

Some developments in Lombardy seem to be inspired more by neoliberal thinking than by subsidiarity. In 2003, for example, the municipality of Milan privatized the management of its 30,000 units public housing stock to a private management company. This outsourcing of public housing management was not successful as this management company underperformed. In 2009, the municipality of Milan decided to re-award the management back to ALER as prior to the outsourcing. This transfer of management could be an opportunity to include clear performance criteria in the agreement between the Milan municipality and ALER.

### 9.3.1.2. Horizontal Subsidiarity

Horizontal subsidiarity is at the core of the Lombard model of governance; it is the principle that civil society actors can very well carry out "public" functions. Government bodies should not stand in the way of these initiatives but rather support society to meet its own needs (IReR, 2009b). In social housing the development of housing cooperatives from the second half of the nineteenth century is a good example of horizontal subsidiarity long before it became a governing principle used by Lombardy Regional Government (only after the Housing Law of 1903 did the government enter the field of social housing provision). Stronger still, housing cooperatives emerged to tackle housing problems ignored by the government.

Housing cooperatives are the major nonstate provider of social housing in Lombardy. Cooperatives are often connected to socialist or Catholic civil society movements. This diversity is still visible in the way housing cooperatives are organized even so many years after their foundation. In Lombardy there are three organizations supporting local cooperatives; one organization has socialist roots; two have a Catholic background. Their connection to civil society is still strong although some observers claim that cooperatives have become too market oriented. The extent of their contribution to social housing provision does not easily show up in Lombard housing statistics, which mainly focus on publicly owned housing.

### 9.3.1.3. Quasi Markets

Quasi markets are an important vehicle for subsidiarity in the Lombard model of governance; the regional government reformed health and education policies to include quasi-market mechanisms. Brugnoli and Vittadini (2009, p. 28) mention three key instruments currently used by the Lombardy Regional Government to create quasi markets:

1. practical pluralism—offered by separating suppliers from programs and separating property from its management;
2. freedom of choice—through the principle of accreditation and quality evaluation; and
3. fiscal subsidiarity—through coupons, vouchers, and tax exemptions and allowances.

We will discuss how these instruments are applied in affordable housing provision.

Pluralism: initiatives to encourage private and nonprofit actors to invest in new affordable rental homes appear to be not very successful. This is due to—at least—two factors: the first, as discussed above, is the limited possibility of making a viable business out of the housing rental market. The second factor is that by using regional subsidies to build rental homes, housing providers are obliged to allocate these houses to candidates on municipal waiting lists. This leaves them very little freedom of choice to select candidates. This goes against the basic principles of some providers, especially housing cooperatives, to build intergenerational housing solutions for their members.

Freedom of choice: the Lombardy Regional Government is contemplating an accreditation and quality assessment mechanism for social housing providers. This idea is still in development, in part, because the number of providers willing to invest and manage social rented housing is still very limited.

Fiscal subsidiarity: the Lombard region has created a voucher system for first-time homebuyers. These families receive a subsidy of

€6,000. Residents in private housing can receive a housing allowance if they can demonstrate that they are in financial difficulty.

### 9.3.1.4. Responsibility

Freedom of choice and responsibility are important elements of subsidiarity for both the demand and the supply sides of services. In the ambit of public services, freedom of choice is often seen as the right of the consumer and the responsibility of the provider. However, there is also the responsibility of the user and the freedom of the provider (Brugnoli and Vittadini 2009, pp. 29–30). In this respect the principle of subsidiarity is still not very well implemented in Lombard social housing practices.

For example, around 15 percent of public housing tenants do not pay their rent (see Table 9.1 above), and 40 percent do not pay the full amount. In addition, a substantial share of the public housing stock is illegally sublet. It is reported that is it very difficult for both private and public landlords to evict tenants with rent arrears. According to the Italian Constitution, housing is a fundamental right and landlords that evict tenants can be ordered by a court to supply—and pay for—alternative accommodation. It is questionable if rights and responsibilities are equally divided between the consumers and providers of social housing services.

As a consequence, social rented housing, but also rented housing in the private sector, is not a very attractive market for providers. This is illustrated by the fact that in the province of Milan alone 80,000 private rental dwellings are empty.

In addition, initiatives of the Lombard region and the city of Milan to attract new nongovernmental providers to the social housing market have not been successful. Private and nonprofit providers such as housing cooperatives are reluctant to develop affordable rental dwellings, let alone social rental housing for the lowest income groups. They only seem to be prepared to include small proportions of social rented housing in their projects if they are "compensated" with considerable numbers of owner-occupied housing. The share of social rental housing in these projects is rarely higher than 10 percent.

The lack of legal leverage with which to enforce rental contracts is a serious problem. This is not an isolated phenomenon, but can also be found in the mortgage market. The average time to foreclosure in Sweden is only 6 months while the average estimated time to foreclosure in Italy is 120 months. Needless to say, the court system in Italy is a serious impediment to the development of both a mature rental housing and mortgage market.

## 9.4. RECOMMENDATIONS

This chapter concludes with some suggestions on the further implementation of subsidiarity in the Lombard social housing sector. These recommendations are grouped around the central principles of subsidiarity.

### 9.4.1. Vertical Subsidiarity

The devolution of power, responsibilities and resources to lower levels of government in social housing could be taken a step further. Housing policy should best remain at a regional level but the management of social housing does not need to be carried out by the regional government. The financial viability and efficiency of the regional social housing agency ALER is problematic as is the management of social housing in general. Housing cooperatives are not very willing to manage housing in the *canone sociale* segment. Even the municipality of Milan shies away from managing its own housing stock. Due to this reserve, ALER is the only de facto operator in the *canone sociale* housing segment. However, an organization that focuses only on housing provision for the lowest-income segment is socially and economically not sustainable. It is socially unsustainable because it can create ghettos and lock tenants into the margins of society, and it is economically unsustainable due to the fact that operating only in the lowest-price segment of the housing market is not viable without a constant flow of government subsidies.

Solving this problem is not easy. A possible way forward is a drastic mission change of public housing providers. One option could be to divide ALER into several nonprofit housing associations, each allocated to a clear geographical zone, and focused on professionally managing the housing stock. Possible role models can be the stock transfers in England and the Netherlands to nonprofit housing associations. Alternatively the housing stock of ALER could be transferred to several publicly owned housing companies that have a high level of autonomy but still are owned and supervised by the region.

The new mission of these organizations should not only be about providing a decent and affordable home, but do this in combination with helping people get on with their lives and help create sustainable communities. In order to do this, the delivery of housing services should be combined with other welfare services, such as vocational training of residents, providing job opportunities and social support, and care for vulnerable people and elderly in sheltered or supported-housing solutions. Social housing operators need not always provide these services themselves; they can also support residents in finding and accessing these services.

## 9.4.2. Horizontal Subsidiarity

The social housing cooperatives in Lombardy are excellent examples of horizontal subsidiarity. Emerging from local communities, they have a long history and have evolved into hybrid organizations that combine affordable housing with housing solutions based on market prices. In addition, they have combined housing with other types of services like sports and theatre facilities and even travel agencies for their members. Residents often self-administrate their homes and housing estates. However, examples of self-administration by residents of housing managed by ALER are rare. Self-administration could be further developed by giving tenants of publicly owned housing the right to take over the management (and possibly even the ownership) of their housing estate if they are able to present a feasible plan—in England, council housing tenants have a legally binding right to do so. The can form Tenant Management Organizations that carry out the housing management activities themselves or outsource these activities to other organizations (see www.nftmo.com).

## 9.4.3. Quasi Markets

With its spatial planning strategy and land policy, the municipality of Milan is creating quasi markets to organize requests for tenders for the development of housing projects. These tenders help to increase the plurality of ideas, products, and providers that is part and parcel of the principle of subsidiarity. This instrument is not without flaws. Some requests for tenders attract very few responses from market parties, sometimes resulting in only a single project proposal being submitted. Proposals often only include a small amount of rented housing with minimal numbers of housing for the lowest-income groups (*canone sociale*). Sometimes, these proposals do include the construction of social housing, but the but not the manage these properties. Actors expect the regional social housing agency, ALER, to acquire and manage the property after construction. As discussed earlier, many investors regard social housing as an unattractive proposition. Investments in social housing could be made more attractive by strengthening the position of landlords in the legal framework.

Increasing the possibilities to enforce lease provisions could make the rental market more attractive and could possibly entice more investors to make use of programs developed by regional and local governments. In addition, it could bring the substantial amount of vacant rental properties in Lombardy back onto the market.

### 9.4.4. Freedom of Choice

The concept of freedom of choice is difficult to implement in a social housing system where demand is much higher than supply and the distribution of housing built with government subsidies is strictly regulated. The current housing allocation mechanism based on waiting lists and indicators for social and economic need (the ISEE) could be made more flexible. At the moment people waiting for an affordable home have little information about the location and characteristics of vacant social housing properties and their chances of being allocated such a house. Possibly the introduction of *choice-based letting* systems could increase transparency and widen freedom of choice. In these systems, used widely operational in the Netherlands and the UK, available properties are published on the Internet or in printed media. Registered candidates can express their interest in one or more of the available dwellings. Selection of the tenant will take place based on the level of urgency, the accumulated waiting time of the candidate, and the characteristics of the dwelling. Choice-based-letting systems can be used to present the available properties of multiple landlords.

Experiences from the Netherlands indicate that choice-based-letting can lead to frustration among candidates if they are constantly unsuccessful in being allocated the home of their choice, and to resistance among landlords if they have no say in the selection of their new tenants. The latter can be solved by giving landlords some discretionary power to select their tenant from a limited number of candidates. The first problem can be addressed by providing information on the results of previous selections, so candidates know the level of urgency, the accumulated waiting time of candidates that were allocated similar dwellings. State-of-the-art Internet-based systems can give candidates a rough estimate of the probability they will be allocated the dwelling of their choice.

Choice-based-letting systems also create a quasi market and provide housing providers with information on the demand for specific housing estates. They can use this information to manage and improve their properties.

To facilitate freedom of choice, the government could introduce performance audit systems for social landlords with outcome indicators based on expectations of customers and other stakeholders (e.g., local authorities). The results of the performance audits can be linked to the access to government subsidies whereby the best-performing organizations are given privileged access to funds available for new housing construction.

### 9.4.5. Public Private Partnerships

Lombardy has a strong civil society and many initiatives illustrate the capability of building networks between government, communities, private, and civil society organizations. Policy initiatives and the creation of new financial instruments, such as a new national housing construction plan (*Piano Casa*) in 2008 and the setting up of a system of housing investment funds in 2009 (*Fondo Investimenti per l'Abitare, FIA*), could create new dynamics and attract new investors to the social housing market. The Lombard region should support and monitor the development of new public-private partnership using these investment funds to develop social rented housing.

### REFERENCES

Brandsen, T., W. Van de Donk, and K. Putters (2005) "Griffins or chameleons? Hybridity as a permanent and inevitable characteristic of the third sector" in *International Journal of Public Administration*, 28(9), 749–65.

Brugnoli, A., and G. Vittadini (2009) *Subsidiarity: Positive Anthropology and Social Organization. Foundations for a New Conception of State and Market and Key Points of the Experience in Lombardy* (Milan: Guerini).

IReR (2009a) *Società, governo e sviluppo del sistema Lombardo: Lombardia 2010, rapporto di legislatura* (Milan: Guerini).

IReR (2009b) "Subsidiarity: Brief anthology" (Unpublished draft) Regione Lombardia.

Kemeny, J. (1995) *From Public Housing to the Social Market, Rental Policy Strategies in Comparative Perspective* (London: Routledge).

Koppenjan, J., and E. H. Klijn (2004) *Managing Uncertainties in Networks: A Network Approach to Problem Solving and Decision Making* (London: Routledge).

Urbani, S., and G. Van Bortel (2009) "Social housing provision in the Italian region of Lombardy: Between market, state and community". Paper presented at the ENHR 2009 conference in Prague.

# CONTRIBUTORS

**Alessandro Colombo** is director of the "Governance and Institutions" Strategic Unit at Éupolis Lombardia, the Lombardy Regional Institute for Research, Statistics, and Training, which provides strategic advice to the presidency of the regional government and supports the presidency's international relations. His research topics are the principle of subsidiarity, Lombard model of governance, policy analysis, and economic and social history.

**Charles L. Glenn** is a professor of educational leadership and former dean of the School of Education at Boston University, where he teaches courses in education history and comparative policy. From 1970 to 1991, he was in charge of urban education and equity for the Massachusetts Department of Education. Glenn has published studies on educational policies in more than forty countries, with a focus on the right to education, especially of language minority groups, and on educational freedom and rights of conscience.

**Dr. Helen Haugh** is senior lecturer at Judge Business School and deputy director of the MBA program. Her research interests focus on social and community entrepreneurship, community economic regeneration, business ethics, and corporate social responsibility. Her research in the social economy has examined community-led regeneration in peripheral rural communities, cross-sector collaboration between organizations in the social economy and the private and public sectors, and innovations in governance. This work has been published in the *Academy of Management Education and Learning, Organization Studies, Entrepreneurship Theory and Practice, Journal of Business Ethics, Cambridge Journal of Economics,* and *Entrepreneurship and Regional Development.*

**Gyula Horváth** is professor in regional economics and policy of the University of Pécs and director of the Centre for Regional Studies, Hungarian Academy of Sciences. He is member of the Academia Europaea (London) and president of the Hungarian Regional Science

Association. His specialized professional competence is European regional policy, restructuring, and regional transformation in Eastern and Central Europe. He has undertaken extensive advisory and consultancy work within Hungary and Europe. He is member of the Evaluation Board of the Framework Programme of the European Commission and external expert in RIS, RITTS, PHARE, and TACIS projects of the European Commission.

**Michael Kitson** is university senior lecturer in global macroeconomics at the Judge Business School, University of Cambridge; knowledge hub director of the UK-Innovation Research Centre; director of the Programme on Regional Innovation at the University of Cambridge; fellow of St Catharine's College, Cambridge; and research associate of the Centre for Business Research, University of Cambridge.

**Dr. Balázs Lóránd** is an assistant professor of the Faculty of Business and Economics, University of Pécs (Hungary). He obtained a PhD degree (*summa cum laude*) in economics from the University of Pécs Regional Policy and Economics Doctoral School. His research topics are regional development, policy evaluation, and public sector. He also works as an advisor in consultancy projects (public management, organizational development, etc.) and as a trainer.

**Dr. Philip Mcdermott** is an independent consultant in local government and urban development matters; a principal of CityScope Consultants Ltd., based in Auckland; and adjunct professor of regional and urban development in the Institute of Public Policy at Auckland University of Technology.

**Lester M. Salamon** is a professor at the Johns Hopkins University and director of the Johns Hopkins Center for Civil Society Studies. Dr. Salamon is a pioneer in the empirical study of the nonprofit sector and of the growing use of indirect tools of action on the part of governments throughout the world. He is the author or editor of more than a dozen books, including *The Tools of Government: A Guide to the New Governance* (Oxford 2002), and *Rethinking Corporate Social Engagement: Lessons from Latin America* (Kumarian 2010). He serves on the Board of the Community Foundation of Anne Arundel County and is a member of the Editorial Boards of *Voluntas, Administration and Society, Society, Nonprofit and Voluntary Sector Quarterly*, and of the Scientific Committee of *Atlantide*, the journal of Italy's Fondazione per la Sussidiarietà.

**Gerard Van Bortel** is a housing researcher at the OTB Research Institute at Delft University of Technology in the Netherlands. He specializes in organizational and institutional developments in social housing and neighborhood regeneration. He is also involved in research related to performance measurement, governance, and accountability of social landlords.

# INDEX

This index does not aim at providing a comprehensive reivew of single quotations. Neither it encompasses all the terms.

Althusius, Johannes 8, 16
Aquinas, Thomas 8, 16
Aristotle 7–8, 16
Australia 74, 76–78, 85–86, 92, 100

Canada 77, 92
Civil society 12, 15, 51, 53, 59–60, 68–69, 73, 80–83, 88, 95, 97–99, 101–6, 114–15, 117–20, 137, 140, 157, 163–65, 170
Common Good 4, 6–7, 11, 26, 75, 137

Decentralization 12, 23, 31–32, 41–49, 52, 57, 67, 70, 73, 102, 121, 130
Democracy 9, 16, 17, 23, 31, 62, 73, 80, 87–89, 91, 94–97, 100, 102–3, 106–8
Desire 5, 11, 58, 61, 93, 132
    see also Subsidiarity, Anthropological Roots
De Toqueville, Alexis 9–10, 16

Europe
    Cohesion policy 32, 37, 40, 46, 48, 49
    European Union 31–32, 34–40, 42, 46–49, 70, 79, 98, 100, 114, 118, 121, 124, 147

Federalism 22, 51–52, 64–65, 132, 138
Freedom of Choice 12–15, 21, 24, 26, 58–59, 71, 82, 95, 98, 101, 118, 122, 127, 129, 131, 133, 136, 139–40, 143, 146, 165–66, 169–70

Health Care 11, 13–15, 21, 25–26, 56, 61, 63–64, 69, 71, 76–77, 81–84, 92, 98–99, 105, 128, 135, 137–46, 155, 165

Locke, John 9, 17

Mill, John Stuart 10, 17

New Zealand 73–74, 78–79, 83–85, 88, 91–92, 95–108

Pluralism 20, 26, 82, 121, 161
Proximity 97, 150, 152–54
Public Private Partnership 11, 170

Quasi-Market(s) 17, 22, 24–30, 51, 58–59, 61, 67–68, 71, 74, 87, 98, 106, 137, 140–41, 143–46, 163, 165, 168–69

Reciprocity 11, 23, 80, 141, 146
Regionalism 31, 40–42, 44, 47, 49, 52, 66, 70, 137
    NUTS system 33–37

Responsibility 4, 9, 10, 14, 17, 28,
    36, 44, 53, 55, 57–59, 63–64,
    69, 76, 80, 85, 89, 104, 106,
    114, 121, 125, 132, 136,
    138–40, 144, 160, 163–64, 166

Solidarity 11, 23, 26, 29, 64–65, 69
State
    New idea of 6–8, 10–12, 20,
        42–47, 52–53, 55, 57–58,
        61–64, 68–69, 74–75, 80–81,
        91, 117–18, 136–37, 146, 157
    State-Society Relations 66–67
Subsidiarity
    Anthropological root 5–6
    Fiscal 15, 64, 82, 165
    History of 3–4, 7–10
    Horizontal 6, 11, 22–23, 33, 45,
        56–57, 71, 73, 75, 79–80, 83,
        93, 97–99, 102–3, 132, 136,
        144, 155, 163, 164, 168

    Vertical 6, 22–23, 73, 75, 79–80,
        83, 93, 98, 102, 136, 144, 155,
        163, 167

Third Sector 15, 27–29, 62, 67–68,
    80, 138, 149, 170
Trust 11, 23, 53, 58, 75, 105–6,
    115, 132, 141, 146, 150, 152,
    154–55

UK 28, 42, 68, 136, 141, 144–45,
    153, 156, 169
United States 9, 23, 25–26, 30,
    68, 76

Voucher
    Buono scuola/Dote (School
        Voucher) 13, 21, 119,
        126–30, 131
    in Lombardy 21, 25, 58, 82,
        126–30, 131